THE MISSOURI STATE PENITENTIARY

MISSOURI HERITAGE READERS

General Editor, Rebecca B. Schroeder

Each Missouri Heritage Reader explores a particular aspect of the state's rich cultural heritage. Focusing on people, places, historical events, and the details of daily life, these books illustrate the ways in which people from all parts of the world contributed to the development of the state and the region. The books incorporate documentary and oral history, folklore, and informal literature in a way that makes these resources accessible to all Missourians.

Intended primarily for adult new readers, these books will also be invaluable to readers of all ages interested in the cultural and social history of Missouri.

OTHER BOOKS IN THE SERIES

Arrow Rock: The Story of a Missouri Village, by Authorene Wilson Phillips

Blind Boone: Missouri's Ragtime Pioneer, by Jack A. Batterson

Called to Courage: Four Women in Missouri History, by Margot Ford McMillen and Heather Roberson

Catfish, Fiddles, Mules, and More: Missouri's State Symbols, by John C. Fisher

Daring to Be Different: Missouri's Remarkable Owen Sisters, by Doris Land Mueller

Five Stars: Missouri's Most Famous Generals, by James F. Muench

Food in Missouri: A Cultural Stew, by Madeline Matson

George Caleb Bingham: Missouri's Famed Painter and Forgotten Politician, by Paul C. Nagel

German Settlement in Missouri: New Land, Old Ways, by Robyn Burnett and Ken Luebbering

Hoecakes, Hambone, and All That Jazz: African American Traditions in Missouri, by Rose M. Nolen

Immigrant Women in the Settlement of Missouri, by Robyn Burnett and Ken Luebbering

The Indomitable Mary Easton Sibley: Pioneer of Women's Education in Missouri, by Kristie C. Wolferman

Into the Spotlight: Four Missouri Women, by Margot Ford McMillen and Heather Roberson

The Ioway in Missouri, by Greg Olson

Jane Froman: Missouri's First Lady of Song, by Ilene Stone

Jesse James and the Civil War in Missouri, by Robert L. Dyer

Jessie Benton Frémont: Missouri's Trailblazer, by Ilene Stone and Suzanna M. Grenz

M. Jeff Thompson: Missouri's Swamp Fox of the Confederacy, by Doris Land Mueller

Missouri at Sea: Warships with Show-Me State Names, by Richard E. Schroeder

Missouri Caves in History and Legend, by H. Dwight Weaver

On Shaky Ground: The New Madrid Earthquakes of 1811-1812, by Norma Hayes Bagnall

Orphan Trains to Missouri, by Michael D. Patrick and Evelyn Goodrich Trickel

The Osage in Missouri, by Kristie C. Wolferman

Paris, Tightwad, and Peculiar: Missouri Place Names, by Margot Ford McMillen

The People of the River's Mouth: In Search of the Missouria Indians, by Michael Dickey

Quinine and Quarantine: Missouri Medicine through the Years, by Loren Humphrey

The Santa Fe Trail in Missouri, by Mary Collins Barile

A Second Home: Missouri's Early Schools, by Sue Thomas

Stories from the Heart: Missouri's African American Heritage, compiled by Gladys Caines Coggswell

The Trail of Tears across Missouri, by Joan Gilbert

THE MISSOURI STATE PENITENTIARY

170 Years inside *The Walls*

Jamie Pamela Rasmussen

University of Missouri Press   Columbia and London

Copyright © 2012 by
The Curators of the University of Missouri
University of Missouri Press, Columbia, Missouri 65201
Printed and bound in the United States of America
All rights reserved
5 4 3 2 1   16 15 14 13 12

Cataloging-in-Publication data available from the Library of Congress.
ISBN 978-0-8262-1987-9

♾™ This paper meets the requirements of the
American National Standard for Permanence of Paper
for Printed Library Materials, Z39.48, 1984.

Cover design: Susan Ferber
Interior design and composition: Jennifer Cropp
Printing and binding: Thomson-Shore, Inc.
Typefaces: Lubalin Graph, Minion, and Stencil

IN LOVING MEMORY OF

I. E. Beard

1906-1992
Missouri State Highway Patrol
1939-1964
Thanks, Grandpa.

CONTENTS

THE MISSOURI STATE PENITENTIARY

Escape!

With whatever precaution, prison escapes always have been occurring, and always will be.—Augustus W. Alexander, secretary of the Missouri State Board of Guardians (1873)

The year is 1905.

Four inmates—Ed Raymond, Harry Vaughan, George Ryan, and Hiram Blake—approach Deputy Warden R. W. See at the Missouri State Penitentiary. To his surprise, the inmates are armed with Colt .44s and explosives. Warden See pulls out his pistol, but the inmates, anxious for freedom, fire first. The warden is wounded in the hand, and the inmates take him prisoner. They demand that he order Captain John Clay to open the prison gates and the men advance, hustling the warden ahead of them and picking up two other hostages on the way.

Captain Clay sees the approaching inmates and quickly takes action. He tosses the keys to a guard on the other side of a heavily barred door. With a shout of rage, Vaughan shoots Clay in the head, killing him instantly. The inmates then rush to another gate, kill the guard there, and set explosives to blast the gate. The first blast fails to leave a hole big enough to crawl through. As the inmates hurry to set a second charge, guards sound the alarm, alerting local police and townspeople.

Finally, the explosions create a larger hole, and the four men wriggle through to freedom. They take off down the railroad tracks that run next to the prison. Shots ring out, and Blake goes down. He's taken to the prison infirmary where he later dies, but the other three escapees reach the railroad depot a few blocks from the prison at the foot of Monroe Street and commandeer a freight wagon. In the wagon, they race down Monroe Street. Police and townspeople shoot at the convicts, and the convicts return fire.

On Dunklin Street, at the Capital City Brewery, it has been business as usual until the telephone rings. The voice on the line warns the president of the brewery, Jacob Moerschel Sr., about the approaching convicts. The brewery employees rush out to watch in fascination and terror: historian Gary Kremer reported in his book *Heartland History: Essays on the Cultural Heritage of the Central Missouri Region* that one of the employees later recalled, "We saw them driving south for some distance, the horses galloping and running at great speed, followed by citizens afoot, and by horse and buggy, exchanging gunfire, Western Movie style." As the wagon full of convicts passes, Moerschel steps out and gets a secure grip on the reins of the wagon's horses. Vaughan raises his gun to shoot, but it doesn't go off. Police rush in to arrest the convicts.

Vaughan, Raymond, Blake, and Ryan were added to the long list of Missouri State Penitentiary convicts who escaped only to be recaptured almost immediately. Ryan, in a bid for leniency, agreed to testify against his confederates. He explained that a released convict had smuggled weapons over the wall for them and that they had planned to hijack a train and blow up the bridges as they went.

Although the details are more fanciful, the escape of November 1905 was only one of thousands of escapes from the Missouri State Penitentiary over its 168-year existence. Such escapes and attempted escapes are born of the eternal struggle between dangerous men and the society they prey upon. Many people feel a fascination with escape attempts, fueled by stories like this. For most of our nation's

This picture shows the hole through which four inmates escaped to freedom in 1905. Ultimately, three of them were hanged for crimes they committed during the escape. On the day of the hanging, newspapers proclaimed that the escapees had been "Jerked to Eternity." Courtesy of Missouri State Archives.

history, this struggle has continued to play out in the courts and the prisons, and the Missouri State Penitentiary has epitomized American prisons.

When asked during a December 2009 interview how the Missouri State Penitentiary compared to other famous prisons, historian and former prison administrator Mark Schrieber said, "It's older and meaner." That short phrase exemplifies the penitentiary's place in history. For 168 years, the Missouri State Penitentiary was everything other prisons were and more. As in many other prisons, the inmates called the institution "the Walls." When convicts across the nation wore stripes and walked in silent lockstep, Missouri's prisoners did the same. When prisons began to hire out convict labor to industry, the Missouri State Penitentiary did the same. In fact, it became one

This view of Housing Unit One was the main entrance of the penitentiary for many years. As the penitentiary grew and changed, the building served many functions. During the first decades of the twentieth century it held the warden's office and the women's unit. Later, the building served as a diagnostic unit for new prisoners. Sometimes the diagnostic unit was so crowded that new inmates had to sleep on mattresses on the floor in the hallways. The façade shown in this picture was covered by a new attached administrative building in the latter half of the twentieth century. The administration building was then removed when the Jefferson City Convention and Visitors Bureau began offering historic tours of the old penitentiary. Photograph by the author.

of the major manufacturing centers in the state. More recently, as inmate lawsuits and soaring inmate populations changed prisons into "correctional institutions," the Missouri State Penitentiary was replaced. Through the stories of the penitentiary's inmates and administrators, this book shows how this old institution was among the foremost examples of the penitentiary system in the United States.

For over a hundred years, beginning around the turn of the nineteenth century, the penitentiary system dominated the way society dealt with those who violated the law. In the penitentiary system, officials imposed solitary confinement and hard labor to reform convicted criminals. This system represented an advance over older systems in that it was based on the idea that men could be reformed. At the same time, however, administrators often did not have the experience to realize their optimistic goals. At the Missouri State Penitentiary, the struggle between prison administrators, with their goal of reforming convicts, and politicians, with their goal of spending less money to support convicts, often shaped policy.

This struggle also shaped the lives of the inmates. At first, the political pressure to make the penitentiary self-sufficient meant prisoners spent long hours at hard labor. Only when rising rates of violence in the prison itself and high numbers of released convicts returning to crime proved that the system was not working did politicians begin to allocate the money needed to support truly reformatory programs. But, ironically, the success of those programs meant the penitentiary system in Missouri had to become something entirely new. The story of that transformation is examined in these pages.

The Founding of the Penitentiary

We were aroused by the rattling of bolts and locks, the slamming of iron doors, with a dismal, hollow sound as it echoed through the hall, and the music of chains . . . —George Thompson, *Prison Life and Reflections*

Many of the reformers who developed the idea of the penitentiary saw it as an institution that would civilize both the inmates it held and the society around it. In its early years, the Missouri State Penitentiary was used in both ways, although not necessarily in the way theorists had planned.

In the American colonial period and in the first years of the existence of the United States, justice was swift and painful. Religion was the bedrock of society, and criminal justice theories reflected that. Crime was equated with sin, so officials found it difficult to recognize gradations in culpability for different offenses. This attitude resulted in an extremely harsh system of punishment. Criminals were punished primarily in physical ways. The death penalty was still used for most serious felonies, including rape, robbery, and murder. For lesser offenses, colonies and early states employed fines, whippings, mutilations, and banishment. Jails were merely places where suspects awaited trial or convicts awaited the execution of their sentences. Reform was not an objective in this era because religious ideas caused people to believe that a person's character could not be changed.

After the American Revolution, a new optimism entered American thinking, and with it, the potential for reform. Society became more mobile and Americans sought ways to stabilize their world. David J. Rothman described the attitudes of this period in his book *The Discovery of the Asylum: Social Order and Disorder in the New Republic.* He said that during this era, "the prospect of boundless improvement confronted a grim determinism." Rothman concluded that reformers began to believe that "to understand why men turned criminal or became insane or were poor would enable reformers to strengthen the social order." Fired by Enlightenment ideals and appalled by the physical brutality of colonial punishments, the activists soon began to develop an entirely different idea of punishment.

In the latter part of the 1700s, societies of reformers sprang up to agitate for the implementation of these new ideas. Although there were at least two major schools of thought regarding the structure this reform should take, all the reformers agreed that they should try to eliminate the causes of crime and that prisons could demonstrate better methods for organizing society.

Out of this thought, two practical characteristics of the penitentiary system took root. The first was the need to isolate the inmate from the pernicious influence of other inmates. In many ways, isolation was the guiding force of the penitentiary system. Inmates at the Pennsylvania Penitentiary spent twenty-four hours a day locked in their cells, each with an individual courtyard for a minimal amount of air and exercise. In other systems, like that employed at the Missouri State Penitentiary, isolation was accomplished simply by prohibiting talking. Without conversation, reformers thought, a man's conscience would become his punishment as his isolation would cause him to reconsider his deeds. The second major pillar of the penitentiary system was hard work. Hard work, reformers believed, would teach the inmates how to earn an honest living after their time in the penitentiary was done. Together, isolation and hard labor formed the core of the penitentiary system.

Two of the earliest penitentiaries were founded in eastern states just as Missouri was struggling for statehood. Auburn in New York was established between 1819 and 1823, and the Pennsylvania Penitentiary was established during the latter 1820s. So when Missouri became a state in 1821 and began setting up a system of government, the new ideas about how to handle society's criminals played an important role.

In 1821, Missouri entered the union as a result of the Missouri Compromise. Under the Missouri Compromise, Missouri was admitted as a slave state while Maine was admitted as a free state to keep the balance between the increasingly hostile northern and southern factions. When the state of Missouri was formed, most of its population was clustered in the eastern portion along the Mississippi River. Fur trading was the most important industry of the new state, and many of the inhabitants of the major towns, including St. Louis, still spoke French rather than English. Land speculation was rife, courts and roads had yet to be established, and Indian raids were still a concern in some areas. It was a wild country, and many called it the "Mother of the West." Settlers streamed in, all of them hoping to make their fortunes.

One of the first major issues faced by the new state government was the selection of a location for the capital city. In selecting the site, Missouri's founding fathers had to balance many interests, including accessibility, cost, and politics. Perhaps the foremost concern was accessibility. Roads were still poor or nonexistent throughout much of the state, and river travel by steamboat was still the most efficient mode of travel. To make the capital more accessible, the drafters of the Missouri constitution declared that the capital of the state had to be located "within forty miles of the mouth of the Osage River on the Missouri."

The new government was also concerned with the cost of setting up house. Because of this, they decided to take advantage of a special grant made by Congress. When Congress enacted the law creating Missouri as a state, it offered four sections of government land for the building of a capital. This limited the location because there were already extensive private holdings in the state from early French and Spanish settlement in the territory.

The new state set up a temporary capital in St. Charles, and short-ly thereafter, the legislature appointed a group of commissioners to select the permanent site. The commissioners set out on an arduous journey to view a number of possible locations. They found that the settlement that would become Jefferson City, at that time hardly a village, was the only location that both complied with the constitu-tional mandate and allowed the state to take advantage of the federal grant. Still, they recommended another site in what is now Callaway County as more favorable. This recommendation might have con-tributed to the prejudice that many felt towards the new town when Governor Frederick Bates chose it.

The capital was officially moved to Jefferson City in 1826, but not everyone was satisfied with the new site. Opponents thought the area was growing too slowly and was too far from major metropolitan areas. Some maintained the capital should and would be moved. A newspaper editor in Columbia wrote regarding Jefferson City, "Na-ture never designed such a spot as a place of commerce, business, or indeed of importance in any other respect—and not a dollar of pub-lic money should be expended in the erection of any public works in it." It would take more than a capitol building to keep the govern-ment in Jefferson City.

Later, Governor John Miller saw the difficulties posed by the un-certainty surrounding the permanent location of the government. A native of Virginia and a veteran of the War of 1812, Miller had made Missouri his home after being stationed near Bellefontaine during Missouri's territorial days. Settling in Howard County, established in 1816 in the Boonslick, he made it his goal to mold the state into an orderly community by building roads, establishing courts, and avoiding political infighting.

Another way Governor Miller sought to cement the establishment of the state was by developing Jefferson City. As part of this plan, he advocated the building of a state penitentiary in the city. In his second biennial address in 1830, the governor stated, "The peniten-tiary system merits the attention of the legislature. The state might gain some advantages by its adoption." He extolled the benefits of the penitentiary system as "more effectual in preventing crime" and cheaper than older systems of confining criminals in county jails. In his third biennial address in 1832, he made the connection between the establishment of a solid seat of state government and the building of a penitentiary in Jefferson City even clearer. He pointed out the problems caused by continual debate over whether Jefferson City should remain the capital, including failure to invest in the city's infrastructure. Then, he spoke of a penitentiary: "The erection of a Penitentiary here, the necessity and utility of which cannot be doubted, would contribute in a great degree to settle the public mind in relation to the permanent location of the Seat of Government." Thus, Governor Miller saw the penitentiary as supporting his goal of building a stable state government in two ways. First, the penitentiary system would encourage the rehabilitation of society's deviants. Second, it would be a substantial investment in the infrastructure of Jefferson City and so would help to cement the city's position as home of the state capital.

The debate about building a penitentiary was not merely a routine aspect of setting up state government. In addition to the general objections against Jefferson City, observers were concerned because most inmates would come from the St. Louis area. The location of the penitentiary became an issue in statewide elections. Boone County residents thought the penitentiary ought to be located in their county as opposed to the capital city. Eventually, Governor Miller was able to gather enough votes for the construction of the penitentiary in Cole County by convincing Boone County politicians that if they voted to locate the penitentiary in Jefferson City, he would support their efforts to have the state university located in Columbia. Later, the governor credited the success of the penitentiary project to the support of Boone County politicians. That success had far-reaching consequences for the state. It was only after the passage of the penitentiary bill that the public stopped agitating for moving the capital.

In January 1833, the Missouri legislature passed a bill appropriating $25,000 for the building of a state penitentiary in Jefferson City.

The legislature expected the construction work to be completed by October 1834. James Dunnica and John Walker oversaw construction, and the facility was completed in 1835. It consisted of a keeper's house, a cellblock, some outbuildings and a strong wall of Missouri limestone. It had forty cells, each with sufficient space for inmates to do independent work such as putting together shoes from pre-cut pieces, and the goal was that prisoners would be reformed though solitary contemplation of their sins and long hours of hard labor.

The first inmate, Wilson Edison, arrived from Greene County in March 1836. He was serving a sentence of two years, one month, and fifteen days for stealing a $39 watch. He was not unlike many early prisoners. Near the end of 1836, all but one of the prisoners had been convicted of grand larceny. Also like many early prisoners, Edison received a pardon after serving only a portion of his sentence. In those days, hope of a pardon was the only chance of early release from the harsh conditions of the penitentiary. Prisoners and their families lobbied for that relief constantly.

The penitentiary system was intended to be difficult both psychologically and physically. In Missouri, legislators also believed that the penitentiary should be financially supported by the labor of the inmates. These two factors quickly made the lives of the inmates at the Missouri State Penitentiary more harsh than planned.

When an inmate arrived at the prison, half his head was shaved and he was put into a prison uniform. It was thought these distinguishing features would make escape more difficult because they would allow a convict to be immediately recognized. Another method of preventing escape was the notorious ball and chain. A prisoner was chained upon his arrival and remained chained until the guards were convinced he did not pose an escape threat. Only then could the prisoner become a "trusty," that is, a prisoner who had been sufficiently reformed that he merited special privileges. Officials removed the chains from trusties, and they could work outside the prison walls.

After his physical transformation, the psychological assault on the prisoner began. First, the new inmate met with the warden, who

In the early days, inmates wore striped uniforms as pictured above. They marched in lines to meals and to work and were not allowed to look up or talk to each other. Courtesy of Missouri State Archives.

usually ranted at the inmate and threatened to beat him if he did not confess his guilt. Then the inmate was transferred to a tiny cell to spend his first night. This was the beginning of the process of isolation and separation that experts believed would prevent inmates from "contaminating" one another with vice.

Although the population of the Missouri State Penitentiary soon required putting more than one man in each cell, silent submissive contemplation was still required. As George Thompson recalled in his book *Prison Life and Reflections*, there were but four rules at the penitentiary:

1. You must not speak to any prisoner, out of your cell, nor to each other in your cell.

2. You must not look up at any visitor—if it is your own brother; if you do, I'll flog you.

3. You must always take off your cap, when speaking to an officer, or when an officer speaks to you.

4. You must call no convict, "Mr."

These requirements dehumanized the convicts and made it easier for guards to impose the harsh discipline that experts of that time felt was necessary.

Night brought no respite. The convicts slept two or three and sometimes more in cells twelve by eight feet. They were provided with one thin blanket per man. As the thick stone walls kept the interior of the prison as chilled as an icebox, prisoners huddled together to try to keep warm but were often unable to sleep for the cold. Meals were bacon, beans, and hard cornbread.

As if these "reformatory" methods were not enough, convict life was made even harder by the lack of funding. There were no state income taxes at that time. Without the revenue provided by income taxes, the resources of the state would not allow simple confinement; the inmates had to work to produce sufficient income to support the prison. Thus, punishment was often tied to failure to work. Politicians such as Governor Daniel Dunklin urged the legislature to abolish whippings and bring the criminal code more in line with the ideal of reform. Still, physical punishment was not only allowed but seen as essential to prison discipline in the 1830s.

Whipping or beating was the most common form of discipline, and it was inflicted regularly, Thompson wrote. The prisoner's hands were tied in front of him so he could not ward off the blows, and he was stripped to the skin before being laid out on the floor in the warden's office. Beatings were administered with either a thick leather strap or a paddle. The paddle had holes in the working end that would raise blisters on the victim's body. The beating continued until the inmate screamed for mercy.

The problem of balancing the goals of reforming criminals and keeping costs low would continue throughout the penitentiary's existence. The concern for cost effectiveness quickly overcame the notion that solitary confinement was the best way to reform prisoners. Back-breaking labor at all kinds of work was the norm. The town around the prison benefited from this labor, but citizens were also fearful of escapes. However, the town and the prison did develop a give-and-take relationship. Inside, prisoners toiled away long, silent years. Outside, leaders and reformers debated the benefits of reform against the cost of guarding and maintaining prisoners. It was a debate that would continue through the next several decades. In fact, during the ensuing years, the uncertain role of the penitentiary allowed the prisoners to play a role in Missouri's Civil War experience.

The Civil War Period

God grant a candle may be lighted in *this prison*, that shall not
cease to burn, till *slavery* shall come to an end. —George Thompson,
Prison Life and Reflections

Like society at large, the Missouri State Penitentiary felt the sec-
tional rumblings of the Civil War many years before actual fighting broke out. Although there were proportionally few slaves in the
capital city, the governing families were generally pro-southern.
Most had migrated to Missouri from southern states such as Virginia, Kentucky, and Tennessee. But in the 1830s and 1840s, pro-Union
German immigrants began to settle in the area. Thus, as civil war approached, Missouri and its capital city were sharply divided.

The controversy over slavery resulted in some unusual prisoners
at the penitentiary, among them a man named George Thompson.
George Thompson was an Illinois minister with strong abolitionist
views. He and two companions, Alanson Work and James E. Burr,
were associated with the Mission Institute in Illinois, a religious establishment for teaching prospective ministers. At that time, Missouri was a slave state and Illinois a free state. In the first weeks of

July 1841, the three men arranged to help several Missouri slaves cross the Mississippi River to Illinois. Thompson, Work, and Burr met with the slaves and selected a meeting place. They were to gather there on a dark evening a few days later. Thompson would wait in the boat while his companions met the slaves.

Prior to the meeting, some of the slaves told their owners of the plan. The slaves then assisted the owners in capturing the abolitionists. Thompson described the capture of his companions in his book about their experiences: "After dark, a number of slaves came to Alanson and James, in the prairie, and pretended they were going with them. They had proceeded but a short distance, when on a sudden, the slave-holders arose out of the grass, with their rifles, and took them prisoners—placing the muzzle of their guns to their breasts, and threatening, 'I will shoot him any how.'" Back at the boat, another slave pretending to seek his freedom approached Thompson. After Thompson spoke with the slave for a moment, the slave signaled his masters, who threatened Thompson and took him prisoner.

Thompson, Burr, and Work were taken to Palmyra, Missouri, where the local prosecutor was faced with a dilemma. There was no law in Missouri that specifically prohibited planning to help a slave cross into a free state, and the slaves the missionaries had tried to help had not actually escaped. Still, the townspeople demanded convictions. In the past, Palmyra citizens had simply driven off preachers who spoke of abolition, but the arrest of the three do-gooders caused a public outcry. While Thompson, Burr, and Work waited in jail, they were called thieves and abolitionists. Citizens of the town employed the term abolitionist with as much fear and loathing as ministers used the word blasphemer. This anti-abolitionist attitude was not limited to small farming communities. During this time period, three men were hanged in St. Louis for assisting slaves in making their way to Canada.

In the fall of 1841, the Palmyra prosecutor brought the three abolitionists to trial on a charge of stealing; they were quickly convicted and sentenced to prison for twelve years. One friend told them the conviction was a blessing, "for if you had been acquitted, you would all have certainly been murdered."

Thompson, the most outspoken of the three, spent just under five years in prison, and the other two somewhat less. Although they were essentially political prisoners, the three abolitionists shared the same food, work assignments, and conditions as the general prison population. They did their best to hold religious services and teach other inmates, sometimes suffering punishment for doing so. Over the years they were in prison, the Missouri legislature enacted a law against enticing slaves to freedom, and many others saw convictions for that offense.

The controversy over slavery continued to haunt Work, Burr, and Thompson as they sought pardons. Legislators came and spoke with them, informing them that the governor would quickly grant a pardon if they would give their word that they would not attempt to free any more slaves. Well-meaning friends convinced the governor that Work and Burr had been led by the more outspoken Thompson. The friends' words must have seemed true to the governor. Even after Work and Burr had been released, Thompson remained, asserting that he would continue to work for the freedom of the slaves "by all lawful means."

Eventually, lobbying secured Thompson's release as well. The decision to release the three abolitionists did not mean an end to the practice of imprisoning those who helped slaves try to escape, however. Prisoner rosters throughout the next twenty years continue to show men with sentences for "decoying slaves" or "enticing off slaves." In 1858, six men were serving sentences for these crimes. More were sent to prison for that offense as the preparations for war continued.

In 1860, Missourians voted overwhelmingly for Stephen Douglas over Abraham Lincoln for president. Claiborne Fox Jackson, an outspoken secessionist from Boonslick, took the governorship in Missouri. In March 1861, a special convention convened to decide the issue of secession, but no one who supported succession was chosen as a delegate. Thus, Missouri was set to remain in the Union as Lincoln was inaugurated.

Still, southern sympathies persisted, especially in the governor's mansion. When Lincoln mustered the troops in April 1861, Governor Jackson replied,

There can be, I apprehend, no doubt that these men are intended to form a part of the President's army to make war upon the people of the seceded states. Your requisition, in my judgment, is illegal, unconstitutional, and revolutionary in its objects, inhuman and diabolical and cannot be complied with. Not a man will the State of Missouri furnish to carry out such an unholy crusade.

Governor Jackson converted the state militia—known as the Missouri State Guard—into a pro-Confederate force, but they were badly in need of supplies. The Missouri State Penitentiary, which at this time was run by political appointees rather than people who specialized in understanding criminals, was put into action to help supply the militia. First, one of the penitentiary workshops began manufacturing cartridges. Later, other workshops began turning out massive amounts of field equipment. Before long, all the factories at the penitentiary were producing materials destined for use by the Missouri State Guard. Prison officials also depleted the prison stores of food and other supplies in their zeal to help organize the militia for Governor Jackson.

In June 1861, fearing a Union attack after a failed effort to reach agreement with Union officer Nathaniel Lyon in a meeting in St. Louis, Governor Jackson packed up the state papers and seal and moved the capital to Boonville. Shortly thereafter, federal gunboats came up the Missouri River and took control of Jefferson City, continuing in pursuit of Jackson as Jackson eventually retreated into Arkansas.

The Union advance brought a change in masters for the penitentiary but not a change in the work. Once Union forces had established control in the capital city, all government officers, including the officers of the penitentiary, were required to take an oath of allegiance. Most of the penitentiary officers refused. After all, only days before they had been providing goods to the Missouri State Guard. All but one of the penitentiary officers was replaced, and Phillip T. Miller, formerly just a clerk, became warden. Now, with federal officers in control, the prisoners were put to work on the city's fortifications, which were built on the hills surrounding the capital. The first was near the prison on the east. Coming west, the prisoners built fortifications along Dunklin Street. A final fort was built overlooking the river at the head of Boliver Street. The penitentiary workshops continued to churn out war supplies, this time for the Union.

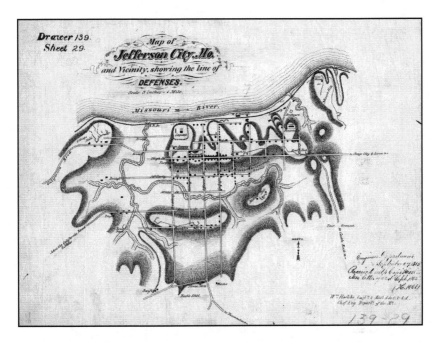

This map depicts Jefferson City as it existed at the time of the Civil War. The bold lines on College Hill, Dunklin Street, High Street, Miller's Hill, and Miner's Hill represent forts built in part using convict labor. This 1865 map is a digital reproduction of a map in the National Archives in Washington, D.C.

As Union forces used prisoner labor to fortify the capital city, Governor Jackson called a meeting of the pro-Southern government in Neosho in southwest Missouri. The legislators of that government ratified the Constitution of the Confederate States of America, and Missouri's government in exile was recognized by the Confederacy. When Jackson died December 6, 1862, in Camden, Arkansas, former governor Thomas Reynolds took responsibility of organizing a capital for the government in exile.

With the pro-Confederacy government in Arkansas, lessening the threat of attack, work on fortifications in Jefferson City ended, and Warden Miller found it difficult to find employment for his five hundred charges. In January 1862, Miller contracted to have many of the convicts provide labor to a St. Louis industrialist named John How. In exchange, How would pay the State of Missouri thirty-five cents per convict per day. Like many wardens before him, Miller hoped that this labor would make the prison self-supporting, if not profitable, for the state.

In 1864, the war again touched the Missouri State Penitentiary. General Order No. 55 moved federal prisoners from Alton, Illinois, to the custody of the Missouri State Penitentiary. The first of these prisoners arrived in June, and they continued to arrive throughout the duration of the war. Many had been convicted in routine courts-martial for offenses such as falling asleep on duty or stealing horses. Others, such as the bushwhackers, were more sensational and showed the divisive forces at work in Missouri.

After the pro-Southern government went into exile, groups of pro-Southern guerrillas known as "bushwhackers" began to spring up throughout the state. These raiders harassed Union troops and tormented civilians who supported the Union cause. Among their numbers were men destined to become some of the most famous outlaws in American history. Jesse James began his career as a bushwhacker following the famous William Quantrill. Quantrill and men like him raided throughout Missouri, stealing horses and supplies, killing troops, burning houses, robbing, looting, and doing what they could to make it difficult for Union troops to operate in the state. While the pro-Southern farmers saw these men as heroes, the Union government labeled them common criminals. Many were shot at the sites of their unsuccessful raids. Those who were lucky enough to be tried and convicted instead were sent to the penitentiary.

Many of the bushwhackers sent to the penitentiary protested they were honest Confederate soldiers. Martin Adams, a private in the Fourth Missouri Cavalry, wrote to protest his innocence of the charge: "Have never bushwhacked, nor would. Have been a regular soldier in the said [Confederate] service and performed no actions against the authority of the U.S. excepting in the regular line of my duty, and in obedience to the orders of my superior officers."

Among the list of prisoners were also spies and those who gave comfort to Confederate forces. The story of Rachel Haynie of Saline County is typical. She provided Confederate guerrillas with food and allowed them to camp on her land. She was found guilty of giving aid to the enemy and sentenced to be confined for the duration of the war. Protests of innocence were common among this type of prisoners as well. Many who were convicted of harboring guerrillas wrote that they were forced to help the rebels on threat of death.

The war effectively ended with the surrender of General Robert E. Lee at Appomattox on April 9, 1865. At the penitentiary, paperwork granting pardons trickled in throughout the rest of the spring. Then, on June 23, 1865, a general order was issued releasing all prisoners who had been sentenced to serve for the duration of the war.

Although the Civil War had caused flurries of activity and at least one drastic change in administration, life for the average prisoner in Missouri did not change much in the war years. Forced labor, small cells, and bad food were the norm. Administrators continued to search for ways to make the prison pay and were astounded by the cost of running it. New administrators spoke of reform as their goal, but economic realities soon overcame those sentiments and paved the way for the factory system.

Earning Their Keep

Occupation facilitates discipline. —Matron of the Missouri State
Penitentiary, Report

In the early days of the penitentiary movement, advocates believed
that prison labor would both allow the prisoners to support themselves and help them to learn industrious habits that would allow
them to become functioning members of society when their prison
sentences were finished. But the push of economic motives created a
different reality. Across the nation, many wardens became preoccu-
pied with plans to develop successful prison industries. And in this
respect, Missouri was the worst of the lot.

In 1839, only three years after the first prisoner arrived at the Missouri State Penitentiary, the Missouri legislature adopted the lease
system. Under this system, the legislature entered into leases with
private businessmen. In exchange for a yearly fee, the businessmen
ran the penitentiary and were permitted to use the labor of the convicts for their own private profit. The first men to take advantage of
this opportunity were William S. Burch and John C. Gordon. The
cost of the lease was $30,000 for five years. As historian Gary Kre-

mer noted in his book *Heartland History*, "Convicts were soon working all over town."

This was perhaps the most visible, and thus most hated, aspect of the lease system. And it caused other problems. Lapses in supervision during work and the practice of working the inmates outside the walls presented numerous opportunities for escape. It seemed that escapes, or at least attempted escapes, occurred on an almost daily basis, horrifying the citizens of Jefferson City. Many believed that the escapes were facilitated by the use of prison labor.

The prison became a center of industry in Missouri as manufacturers moved their businesses to Jefferson City to take advantage of cheap inmate labor. During the first century of the penitentiary's existence, inmates toiled from dawn to dusk in workshops like the broom factory shown above. Courtesy of Missouri State Archives.

In fact, the first large-scale prison break at the Missouri State Penitentiary was made possible in part because the warden had left the prison to supervise a work party. On June 14, 1841, Gordon took a large group of prisoners into downtown Jefferson City to work on a building, leaving the overseer, Mr. Bullard, in charge. Three inmates overpowered Bullard in the saddle shop, beat him to death, and stole his keys before joining six other inmates in a rush for the gate. The town rallied to recapture the men but could not stop them from ransacking a local home.

In 1842, the editors of a local newspaper, the *Jeffersonian Republican*, lamented it would be better not to punish crime at all than "to bring a collection of criminals here to roam our hills and through our city, in the performance of various labors and evocations which as a right the lessees [sic] can direct them." Even so, the negative media attention was not enough to motivate the businessmen in charge of the penitentiary to improve the situation. All aspects of the prison had become motivated by business interests. As the men who leased the penitentiary were charged not only with working the prisoners but also with the task of their care and rehabilitation, punishment became tied to work performance. Additionally, the work was frequently dangerous. Safety precautions in the factories of the time were almost nonexistent, and it was worse in the penitentiary. Prisoners were often hurt in the course of their work, and poor medical care resulted in further harm. For example, in the 1840s, George Thompson, a prisoner who wrote a book about his experiences in the penitentiary, reported that when one prisoner's arm got caught in the machinery and was broken, the part-time doctor was not on hand to properly set the bone, and the prisoner had difficulty using his hand for the rest of his life.

Citizens complained that Burch and Gordon were mistreating the prisoners, and their lease was not renewed in 1843. When they knew that their lease would not be renewed, Gordon and Burch stopped spending money on essentials. Prisoners were not even afforded a change of clothes, and conditions became even more brutal. The second lease was to Ezra Richmond and James Brown, and they took possession of the prison on February 16, 1843. They found it in a dreadful condition and initially promised reforms. But the press of business soon led them to disregard these ideas.

Although Richmond and Brown agreed not to work the inmates outside the walls, they soon found ways to avoid this restriction. The lease was amended to allow the prisoners to work on building an extension of the walls, which necessarily required them to leave the yard. Richmond and Brown stretched this rule to its breaking point. They interpreted the rule to include procuring materials for working on the walls or for other work within the walls. Under that interpretation, inmates could work in quarries or forests far from the prison site. Escapes and unrest continued, punctuated with major revolts in 1857 and 1860.

In the 1870s, complaints about abuse of prisoners and the continued failure of the prison to pay its own way resulted in the end of the lease system. However, it was still necessary to employ the prisoners both to help defray costs and to prevent the psychological harm caused by solitary, idle confinement. In 1875, Missouri allowed the final lease to expire and adopted the contract system, under Warden John P. Sebree. In this system, the care of the prisoners was vested in the warden, and the state then contracted out the labor of prisoners. The first contract went to James Price, who paid the state for the privilege of working 150 convicts at his coal mine in Pettis County.

Friction between the free coal miners in neighboring Montserrat and the prison labor in Pettis County presaged the conflict that would plague the contract system. In 1877, coal miners working for the Montserrat Coal Company formed an anti-convict-labor group protesting the cheap cost of convict labor that drove down their wages. However, when the workers eventually went on strike, the managers contracted with the state to use convicts at Montserrat as well.

Back inside the walls, a concerted effort was needed to prepare the prison for the contract system. When he took control after the businessmen left, Warden Sebree found the prison unfit for profitable employment of the inmates. The major problems were the lack of a ready market for inmate labor in Jefferson City—which was too far from the commercial centers of the state—and the lack of space for workshops within the walls. Warden Sebree began a building campaign, improving the existing structures and building more.

By the 1880s, there were half a dozen factories operating within the prison walls. Companies paid between 40 and 45 cents per day for the labor of a convict. The prisoners made shoes, saddle trees, twine, and clothing. Along the streets leading to the prison, factory owners and their families lived in elegant mansions built using convict labor. By 1879, most of the prisoners were employed and for the first time in its history, the Board of Inspectors claimed the Missouri State Penitentiary was self-supporting.

Although companies earned tremendous profits based on the low cost of prisoner labor, the system had some sinister costs. Many inmates resented being forced to work. Efforts to damage the shops were frequent and physical punishment, including whipping, to coerce compliance was commonplace.

One of the most intractable prisoners was named John Johnson. He came to the penitentiary in 1882 to serve a twelve-year sentence for robbery. The sheriff who delivered Johnson to the warden warned the warden "that Johnson was a bad man and would cause trouble." As if that warning wasn't enough, the sheriff reported that Johnson had beaten a county jailer almost to death during an escape attempt. At first, Johnson went to work in the shops as he was told, but six months after his arrival, he made his first attempt to escape by scaling the walls with his cell mate. When they were caught, they were whipped and sent back to work in the harness shop.

But Johnson was not to be deterred so easily. A few months later, he conspired with three other inmates in a more elaborate escape attempt. He and his confederates set fire to the shops, distracting the guards so that they could escape. The result was described many times in subsequent years. In 1894, when Johnson was dying of tuberculosis, a reporter from the *Jefferson City Daily Tribune* remembered the drama of Johnson's famous escape attempt:

> While the other convicts were at dinner Johnson overpowered
> an inside guard and compelled him to make a hasty exchange of

clothing. Meantime his companions had set fire to the shop and cut the prison hose. Johnson, being dressed in citizens' clothes, and having bound and gagged the guard, rushed to the large gate next to the Missouri river and started to climb up a ladder to the guard house with a view of overpowering the guard, securing his gun and pistols and then opening the gate and letting the convicts out. He thought that the guard would mistake him for one of the new prison officers. But here his plan failed. The guard was an old officer and immediately presented his gun and Johnson's game was up.

Stopping the convicts was not the only challenge officials faced that day. In preparing the fire, the inmates had outdone themselves. They employed heaps of kindling and gallons of gasoline. The fire soon raged out of control, and many shops were severely damaged. After the fire, Johnson got a new nickname: Firebug.

Firebug got a reprieve from the shops. The harness shop where Firebug had been employed was so severely damaged that it had to be completely rebuilt. After that, not a single contractor would allow Firebug anywhere near his shops.

Even so, Firebug's career was far from over. The warden kept him in solitary confinement after the fire, and Firebug used his time to write letters to newspapers and a memoir of his time in the penitentiary that he called *Buried Alive; or, Eighteen Years in the Missouri Penitentiary*. Some sources suggest he even wrote a novel, although if he accomplished that, the manuscript did not survive. Over the remainder of his term, Firebug's letters to public officials frequently made the news, even if his tales of whippings and mistreatment were exaggerated.

Although he was one of the more famous rebels, Firebug was not the only prisoner to rebel against the system of forced labor, and constant solitary confinement for over a thousand prisoners was not feasible. To make the system work, officials, like the leasees before them, resorted to various types of punishment. One report noted that the two most common forms of punishment were "whipping with a common riding cowhide and confinement in the dark cell, in

Firebug Johnson. After setting fire to the saddle shop, Johnson made headlines throughout his stay at the penitentiary by writing letters to newspapers and public officials decrying the deplorable conditions he encountered in the penitentiary. When one journalist investigated, he found Johnson's tales of brutality to be somewhat exaggerated. Courtesy of Missouri State Archives.

which a convict is placed and allowed only bread and water." Generally, punishments were inflicted for failing to complete the work assigned by the contractors.

As the 1880s progressed, the prison teetered on the edge of financial success, some years registering a profit and some years not. The population of the prison continued to grow, and the warden had difficulty finding sufficient room to put all the prisoners to work. In 1885, the warden reported finishing an extension of the walls, only to request a further extension to accommodate a continually growing inmate population. Like the leasees before them, the state-employed officials began to suggest working the inmates outside the prison walls.

Another difficulty faced by the prison administrators was a growing public opposition to the use of inmate labor for private profit. In 1890, a former inmate of the Kansas State Penitentiary, John N. Reynolds, was granted permission to visit and write about the Missouri Penitentiary. In the book he wrote after his visit, *The Twin Hells: A Thrilling Narrative of Life in the Kansas and Missouri Penitentiaries*, he called prison labor "the worst form of human slavery." Although he believed it was important for the inmates to have work to occupy their time, he thought the system was flawed because the contractors got rich from the forced labor of the inmates and the system was plagued by political intrigue. Additionally, convicts were still harshly punished if they did not complete their assigned work. Flogging and solitary confinement continued to be common modes of punishment. Reynolds concluded, "The contract system is wrong, and should not have a place in any of the penal institutions of the country." According to Reynolds, "So far as reformation is concerned, the Missouri Penitentiary is a dismal failure."

But the system continued because the use of convict labor brought many advantages to businessmen. In 1891, a law was passed requiring that prison factories be subject to inspection like ordinary commercial factories. Six out of the seven contractors who employed inmates refused to comply and faced no consequences. The penitentiary contractors also had another advantage over those who employed free labor—they did not have to pay rent or utility costs for their shop space as it was included in the cost of the inmate's labor.

These favorable concessions drew businessmen from across the nation. The stories of some of the famous men who used convict labor in their companies read like a description of the American dream. One of the most prominent companies to do business using convict labor from the Missouri State Penitentiary was the Priesmeyer Shoe

Company. Its founder, August Priesmeyer, had been born in Prussia in the winter of 1832 and emigrated to the United States at the age of seventeen. He first settled in Cincinnati, where he learned the shoe trade before moving to St. Louis and going into business for himself in 1869. In 1874, he came to Jefferson City and started a shoe company with a friend, F. Woesten. The pair began business with thirty-five convict laborers; by 1900, the business was so successful that it employed 250 convicts and had salesmen in most states.

As the turn of the century came around, labor agitators in other central Missouri towns called Jefferson City "the convict labor town." And with good reason—many Jefferson City fortunes were made on the backs of convict labor. The company owners lived in mansions—built by prisoners—along Capitol Avenue next to the prison. There they hosted lavish parties, and some allowed their children to ride their ponies in the streets. From these mansions, the businessmen who employed convict labor exerted pressure on politicians in the state capitol at the other end of Capitol Avenue to continue the contract system.

Such lobbying was necessary. Organized labor had joined the chorus of those protesting against the use of prison labor. So-called free labor—ordinary factory workers—resented the sale of cheap prison goods because it depressed the prices for other goods. As one organizer complained in an 1885 letter to the editor of the *Kirksville Weekly Graphic*, "The tendency of this system is to ruin one trade after another and bring all to the convict level." Another wrote to the *Jasper News* over a decade later in 1891 that "Missouri ought not to force honest men to compete with convict labor." Instead, these reformers suggested that convicts be put to work building and maintaining the public roads. But the pressure from company owners forced the continuation of the contract system as well as the adoption of contracts with rates that were very favorable to the businessmen.

In 1913, prisoners who were unhappy with the meals served in the penitentiary staged a mutiny. They refused to leave the dining hall, chanting, "Fry us some meat!" Even though the inmates were eventually talked into returning quietly to their cells, media attention remained focused on the prison. Reports got out that whipping was still a common punishment for those who did not meet the production quotas set by the companies.

These abuses helped organized labor gather the legislative support they needed to end the contract system. In 1917, the state legislature adopted a law prohibiting the use of convict labor for profit by private companies. After that, the warden employed inmates on farms in the surrounding area, growing food to feed themselves, and the factories were converted to manufacture goods for the use of state agencies. Theories of how to deal with prisoners changed, focusing more on rehabilitation and scientific theories of punishment. The prison was moving toward reform.

Women Prisoners Who Changed
the Walls from the Inside Out

I find no criminals among them, but only unfortunates, broken, hapless, and hopeless human beings. —Emma Goldman, *Living My Life*

Institutional reforms often have unexpected beginnings. In the Missouri State Penitentiary, a major impetus for reform in the early 1900s came from a long-neglected aspect of the penitentiary: its wing for female prisoners.

The women's wing of the Missouri State Penitentiary demonstrated the nation's thinking about how to deal with criminals. In the 1800s, when the penitentiary system was at its most popular, almost no thought was given to the problem of dealing with women who had committed crimes. At that time, popular culture conceived of women as morally superior to men, and as a result, people thought that no prisons were needed for women. Documents concerning the problems faced by women convicted of crimes in the nineteenth century are so rare that a definitive historical study, *American Prisons: A History of Good Intentions* by Blake McKelvey, does not even mention such problems. Although women did not always live up to society's expectations, women's duties as mothers and caretakers often made it necessary to secure pardons for them.

In Missouri during the first decades of the penitentiary's existence, this combination of ideology and economic necessity resulted in neglect when women were convicted of serious crimes and sent to the penitentiary. Later, after fits and starts of reform, female prisoners were transferred to a separate site. But the story of the women prisoners in the interim is one of tragedy and transcendence.

When the penitentiary at Jefferson City was first designed and built, it had no separate facilities for female prisoners. For the first five years of its existence, not a single woman was sentenced to serve a prison term. Authorities managed to avoid the problem of creating facilities for women at the prison.

The first woman to be sentenced to a prison term in Missouri was Rebecca Hawkins in 1841. After many years of "cruel and barbarous" treatment, Hawkins attempted to poison her husband. She confessed to the attempted murder and was convicted. Before she could be transferred to the penitentiary, however, another person succeeded where she had failed: Mr. Hawkins was murdered. With their father dead and their mother headed for the penitentiary, the eight Hawkins children were left without a caretaker or provider. Governor Thomas Reynolds took pity on the family and pardoned Hawkins before she reached Jefferson City, making it possible for officials to avoid the problem of women prisoners for a little longer.

When the next Missouri woman was convicted of a crime and received a prison sentence, there were still no facilities for women prisoners. The governor received a number of petitions for her pardon, and she, too, quickly received one.

The third female convict in Missouri was not so lucky. Martha Casto arrived at the penitentiary on August 10, 1843. This time the wardens employed the woman as a domestic servant in their homes. Another prisoner of the time chronicled Casto's sad story, explaining that she was so mistreated by the wife of one of the wardens that she ran away. When Casto was recaptured, she was placed in a cell in the prison and kept isolated there twenty-four hours a day. Of course, guards were allowed in her cell, and Casto later became pregnant and gave birth to a child within the prison walls. Once again, maternal duties motivated leniency. Because prisoners were not allowed stoves in their cells for fear of fire, many members of the public were concerned that Casto's baby would become sick during the winter. On December 6, 1844, mother and child were pardoned.

Unfortunately, Casto's treatment set the standard for the next several years. No separate facilities for female convicts were built. The leasees hired women prisoners out as domestic servants to avoid the spectacle of women working at hard labor alongside male convicts. At night, the women returned to the penitentiary where guards locked them in their cells to keep them from socializing with the male convicts.

The abuses permitted by this system eventually led Governor Meredith Marmaduke to ask the general assembly to build a separate cell block for women prisoners. An effort to turn the warden's home into a female prison failed, and female prisoners continued to be kept in solitary confinement, early pardon their only hope for relief. It wasn't until 1861 that a separate cellblock was built for female prisoners. Even then, the women's cellblock was only the upper story of a building erected to serve other purposes. It had a matron's room, a hospital room, a work room, and seven cells that were designed to accommodate four prisoners each.

Once judges learned that there was a place for women in the penitentiary, they became less hesitant to sentence women criminals to serve time in prison. Very quickly, the female department became overcrowded. As the warden reported in his yearly report for 1866, "The female prison is entirely inadequate to the purposes of that department." In 1871, the next warden reported to the legislature that "the female department has been as well conducted as was possible under the circumstances," and recommended completely separate facilities.

By this time, officials had abolished the practice of sending the women to work outside the walls, but even with a separate cellblock, it was still impossible to prevent contact with male prisoners. Social meetings between male and female prisoners were seen as an impediment to prison discipline, and the inability to completely separate the two groups was seen as a major obstacle to keeping order. Prison officials continued to request funds for the construction of a completely separate prison for female offenders.

By 1873, the women's wing of the prison was extremely over-crowded—a total of forty-nine women were crammed into a space that was designed to hold only twenty-eight prisoners. However, political overseers did not agree with the warden's reports; just the year before the Missouri Board of Guardians reported that the female prisoners were "too few to justify the erection of a new and special prison." Although a separate building for the female department within the prison walls was erected in 1875, improvements continued to be limited.

During the latter half of the 1870s, when the contract system came to the penitentiary, the women prisoners were put to work inside the walls. First, the women were assigned to make prison clothes for themselves and the male convicts; later they sewed overalls and jackets for private contractors. The work was arduous and the women were not permitted to speak during the work day. As most of the women were young and poor, they were easily terrorized by the young factory foreman and the formidable old matron. For many years, the women continued sewing in silence. The inspectors reported the need for more space, but nothing was done. It was the voice of a female inmate in the 1920s that galvanized officials into making better provisions for the treatment of prisoners, first for the women and then for the penitentiary population as a whole.

Kansas-born Kate Richards O'Hare had long been an activist. She originally trained as a teacher but soon tired of the work and began helping her father in his machine shop where she was introduced to union organizing. She later became a leading socialist spokeswoman with national influence. As the United States faced the prospect of war in 1917, O'Hare was convinced that the war could do nothing but hurt ordinary people, and she spoke openly of her beliefs. Later, when the Sedition Act of 1918 made this a potentially hazardous course by providing criminal penalties for expressing a negative opinion of the war effort, O'Hare persisted. Aware that federal authorities were investigating her activities, she sometimes even sent them complimentary tickets to her lectures. Eventually, one of O'Hare's speeches resulted in criminal charges brought against her.

The challenges Kate O'Hare and her husband faced during and after her trial are recounted in detail in *Rebel Against Injustice: The Life of Frank P. O'Hare* by Peter H. Buckingham. Kate O'Hare and her husband did not believe she would be convicted—as he put it, "We lived under the illusion that the Bill of Rights 'protected' something." The couple was shocked when O'Hare was sentenced to serve a five-year federal sentence. When the judge imposed sentence, he called the thin mother of four "the apostle of despair." O'Hare and her husband hired a lawyer for an appeal, but they had underestimated the fear that had prompted the passage of the Sedition Act. O'Hare's appeal was denied, and she took the train from St. Louis to Jefferson City on April 14, 1919, to begin serving her sentence.

In her first letter from the penitentiary, O'Hare wrote to her husband, "I have either much more poise, courage and strength of character than I dreamed of possessing or I am psychologically stunned." As she described conditions to her husband, she began thinking of ways to improve the prison. She noted, "Food is a problem. The kitchen is three blocks from the women's dining hall, and everything is stone cold when served and is uneatable [*sic*]." Instead of complaining further, she noted that she was allowed to keep in her cell any food that did not need to be cooked and asked her husband to make arrangements for her to have an account with a grocer in town.

During her first weeks at the prison, O'Hare met Emma Goldman, who had been sent to the penitentiary a few years earlier for advocating anarchy and the use of birth control. O'Hare was a socialist rather than an anarchist, the two women became friends and together tried to help their fellow inmates, each in her own way. Emma Goldman was a motherly figure; she listened to the other prisoners' problems and helped them obtain things like candy and cigarettes that could make their lives more bearable. O'Hare wanted to change the whole system.

At the same time that O'Hare sought to ensure better food for the women prisoners, she also advocated improvements in the standards of hygiene she found in the penitentiary. O'Hare's letters express outrage at the lack of cleanliness she discovered. In those days, syphilis was a common disease. At the prison, women who had contracted

Kate Richards O'Hare. O'Hare inspired many reforms at the Missouri State Penitentiary through her letter writing. After she was released she continued to agitate for prison reform and eventually worked for the California Department of Corrections. Courtesy of Rare Book, Manuscript and Special Collections Library, Duke University.

syphilis were not separated from those who had not. In fact, all the female prisoners bathed in the same tub once a week, and several women who were infected with other communicable diseases were allowed to work in the kitchen.

With the help of her husband, O'Hare spoke out. She contacted the warden and, when he was unresponsive, wrote letters to public officials, including the federal prison inspectors. On the outside, her husband published her letters in a bulletin to help arouse public support for her plight. O'Hare's accounts of the conditions in the Missouri State Penitentiary were published across the nation. Emma Goldman joked with O'Hare that she wasn't sure whether O'Hare's husband in St. Louis or her access to the press was more valuable in effecting change.

O'Hare's efforts paid off. The dining room was cleaned and got a coat of paint. Meals began to be served hot, and showers were installed so that the women did not have to share bath water. As she worked to improve conditions inside, O'Hare studied the women around her and began to wonder about the causes of crime.

At first, her attempts to get to know her fellow prisoners were rebuffed because they perceived her as more sophisticated than they were. In their words, she was "a lady." As O'Hare wrote to her husband on April 20, 1919, "Our little world has its comedies, its vanities, its classes and its castes, just like the big world outside . . . and the 'politicals' are the aristocracy. Next in rank are the women who have disposed of undesirable husbands." The lowest class in the prison were those who had committed petty crimes like theft and prostitution. Still, the stories of these women and their subsequent treatment began to change the way O'Hare thought about the world.

O'Hare went on to publish a book about her experience at the Missouri State Penitentiary. There, she noted, "The women themselves were, of course, the vividly interesting feature of my prison life." When she entered the prison, O'Hare planned to record the stories of the prisoners she met in a kind of social history. Although penitentiary officials were reluctant to allow her to complete the work, O'Hare was still able to record many stories. Most of the stories were tragic, such as that of a woman O'Hare mentions only as Alice. Alice was a Native American from Alaska who had been hired by a young soldier to take him on a canoe trip. The soldier raped Alice, and she contracted syphilis. According to O'Hare, Alice "reacted according to her tribal custom." She killed the soldier. As a federal prisoner, Alice was sent to serve her time at the federal prison in Kansas. Later she was transferred to the Missouri State Penitentiary because Missouri offered to house federal prisoners for less money than other states.

After talking to several of the poor wretches who had "disposed of undesirable husbands," O'Hare had this observation:

> They were not only the most intelligent of the state prisoners, but they were the exact opposite of what one would natural-

ly think a husband-murderer would be. They were practically all middle-aged, some quite old, and they were quiet, diffident, toil-worn women; the type that bears children uncomplainingly and endures poverty and hardship, neglect and brutality. Then, some day, there is laid upon their burden the last straw. The repressed emotions, the outraged love, the mother ferocity that makes a woman fight for her young, flame into rebellion; taut nerves snap, a man is killed, a home broken up, children scattered and branded; and a woman enters the living tomb of a prison—to be forgotten. And usually she stays there until death ends her misery. . . . The prison doors close behind her—and the world forgets.

O'Hare found herself sympathetic to the problems the women faced. She believed that most of the women's crimes were "wrongs of stupidity and ignorance," not malice. As she stated in her book, "I was never able to discover the expected physical marks of the 'criminal type,' . . . The only stigmata that I could discover were those of poverty, excessive child-bearing, undernourishment, and overwork." Most women were sentenced for crimes involving theft and prostitution, crimes that they had been driven to by poverty and lack of opportunity. O'Hare wrote that she was "quite sure that one-fourth of the women were paying the price, not for their own transgressions, but for those of the men they loved."

As Kate O'Hare came to know the women, she became even more dedicated to improving prison conditions. Her letters to her husband are filled with requests for books she could share with her comrades. Her husband's decision to publish her letters kept her cause in the public eye. Eventually, O'Hare's efforts prompted a visit from federal prison inspector J. F. Fishman. After discussing the situation with the warden and conducting a cursory investigation, Fishman found that many of O'Hare's complaints—such as the poor food and hygiene and the lack of reading material—had been addressed. But that did not mean the visit was fruitless.

In 1920, O'Hare's sentence was commuted to time served, and she devoted the remainder of her life to prison reform. She made a dashing figure, sometimes speaking wearing the cheap dress she had been given upon her release from the penitentiary. In the summer of 1920, she told a writer from the *New York Call* said that the dress made her feel "like a Christmas tree" but she also thought it helped highlight the plight of prisoners.

The attention she had brought to the prison continued to have effects. The combination of O'Hare's activism and Fishman's visit had more far-reaching effects than cleaning up the dining room. After Fishman's investigation, the calls for improvements in the accommodations for women prisoners was taken up by the legislature. Official penitentiary reports in the 1920s continued to suggest a separate facility for the women prisoners. According to officials, this would decrease the opportunities for "unwholesome" conversation between the male and female prisoners, and allow for more precise attention to the unique difficulties women prisoners faced.

In 1926, the women's division of the Missouri State Penitentiary was moved to Prison Farm No. 1. Although still within sight of the penitentiary walls and still under the administrative control of the warden, the move did improve conditions dramatically. The women were housed in dormitories in a converted farm house, and their work at the sewing machines was replaced with canning and other farm-related activities. Officials still thought an entirely separate facility was needed, but after 1926, women were no longer routinely imprisoned behind the great limestone walls in Jefferson City.

The story of women at the Missouri State Penitentiary would not be complete, however, without mentioning one of the most famous female prisoners, and the only woman ever to be executed at the penitentiary. The last female prisoner to be housed at the penitentiary was Bonnie Brown Heady, and she stayed for only a month in 1953.

Bonnie Heady was a prostitute from Kansas City who had definitely seen better days. After her husband died, she entertained her customers in her suburban home to earn the money to pay her bills. That's how she met Carl Austin Hall, who had already served a term in the penitentiary and who made his living robbing taxis. They quickly developed a relationship, and Hall began to act as Heady's pimp.

During the summer of 1953, Hall began his efforts to convince Heady to help him with a kidnapping, explaining to her that the plan would make enough money to allow them to start their lives over. Hall thought the money they could earn through one kidnapping would make all their dreams come true. At first, Heady was reluctant to join the plan, but she had fallen in love with Hall, and her feelings for him made her vulnerable to his persuasive efforts. Hall assured her that he would take all the blame if they were caught. She eventually agreed, and Hall chose as their target Bobby Greenlease, the son of a wealthy car dealer from the Kansas City area.

On September 28, 1953, Heady picked the boy up at his school, telling school administrators that she was his aunt and his mother was ill. Bobby did not know Heady, but he left with her willingly. "He was so trusting," Heady later said. The three then drove out to the countryside where Hall shot the boy in the head and buried him in a shallow grave. Afterward, Hall delivered his ransom note, which demanded $600,000 in $20 bills. Hall figured that was the amount of cash he could carry without difficulty. When Hall made his demand,

Carl Austin Hall, center, convinced his lover Bonnie Heady to help him kidnap Bobby Greenlease. Heady agreed because at first Hall told her Bobby was his own son from a previous relationship. Courtesy of Missouri State Archives.

Bonnie Heady, pictured above, posed as Bobby Greenlease's aunt so the nuns at the boy's school would allow her to take him with her. Later she expressed her remorse to reporters, remembering how the trusting child held her hand as they left the school. Courtesy of Missouri State Archives.

the Greenlease family believed Bobby was still alive. At that time, the FBI had an almost perfect record with respect to getting kidnap victims home alive. Given these two facts, the Greenlease family assembled the cash and arranged to deliver it to Hall.

The transfer of the money took place exactly as planned, but once he had the cash in hand, Hall panicked, and his plan began to unravel. Hall and Heady sped to St. Louis. Hall dumped Heady, already drunk beyond awareness, in a hotel room, got a cab, and asked the driver where he could find a girl, paying exorbitant amounts; both the cab driver and the prostitute he procured began to scheme to get control of the two suitcases filled with cash. In less than twenty-four hours, the cabbie had spoken with two St. Louis police officers who arrested Hall at a local motel. Hall talked, and investigators found

Heady still waiting in the room where Hall had left her. Only half of the ransom money was recovered, and both of the kidnappers were convicted.

Hall and Heady were sentenced to death. Because there was no death row for females, Heady was sent to the penitentiary along with Hall. Neither decided to appeal, and justice was swift. The pair arrived at the penitentiary in November 1953, and their execution was scheduled for December 18. Both were placed in cells on death row.

During their last days, both Hall and Heady spoke with reporters and investigators on multiple occasions. To the reporters, they confessed their remorse. To investigators, they confessed their ignorance about what had happened to the other half of the ransom money. When they weren't being interviewed, Hall read westerns and Heady did crossword puzzles. They were executed together, and their last words were whispered I-love-yous.

Although her fate was perhaps more tragic, the last female prisoner was characteristic of many of the women who had gone before her. Like the women whose stories Kate Richards O'Hare reported, Heady became involved in crime because of her relationship with a man. As Hall said, "I'm the guilty one. She couldn't say no to me. The only sin she was guilty of was loving me." Also like the women Kate O'Hare knew, Heady's problem wasn't crime but poverty. She drank to numb the pain, eventually making horrible choices out of the dangerous mix of dreams and desperation.

Pretty Boy Floyd

I'm not as bad as they say I am, they just wouldn't let me alone after I got out.—Charles "Pretty Boy" Floyd, quoted in Jeffery S. King, *The Life and Death of Pretty Boy Floyd*

Some of the most famous inmates who spent time in the Missouri State Penitentiary did not become famous until after their stay in the penitentiary. One of these prisoners was Charles "Pretty Boy" Floyd. Before going to prison, Floyd was just a small-time criminal. His exploits after his release made him a legend.

Charles Floyd was born on February 3, 1904, in Georgia where his father was a poor farmer. In 1911, the family moved to Oklahoma, and Floyd grew up listening to and reading tales of the famous outlaws of the old west. Floyd quit school at the age of fourteen and started work, first as a harvest hand and later in the oil fields. At night, he frequented local bars where he drank so much Chocktaw beer that his friends called him "Chock." Floyd loved fast cars and chasing girls, and manual labor did not provide the income he needed for those pursuits. In May 1922, Floyd committed his first burglary.

Although his accomplice in the burglary testified for the state, Floyd was able to win an acquittal because his father testified and provided an alibi for the young man. Floyd's father probably hoped that this scrape would be the last. For a time, it seemed that might be the case. Floyd married a local farmer's daughter, Ruby Leonard Hargraves, on June 28, 1924, and tried to make a living as a farmer. By the summer of 1925, though, he was restless. He traded five gallons of whiskey for a pistol and set off to St. Louis with a man he had met during his work as a harvest hand. The pair held up a payroll clerk and got away with over $11,000. As Jeffery King recounted in *The Life and Death of Pretty Boy Floyd*, the clerk told reporters, "The fellow who carried the gun was a mere boy—a pretty boy with apple cheeks." Floyd and his accomplice were later captured because of their lavish spending, and the name stuck.

Floyd pleaded guilty to the payroll robbery in November 1925. He was sentenced to five years in the Missouri State Penitentiary and arrived there on December 18, 1925. The penitentiary was a rough place then, and some people believe that the harsh conditions there contributed to Floyd's later life of crime.

When Floyd arrived at the penitentiary, there were more than three thousand inmates imprisoned behind its walls. They worked twelve hours a day, and the guards whipped them when they did not obey. Prisoners did have the hope for an early release, though. At that time, a prisoner's release date was calculated based on the five-twelfths rule. Under that rule, each inmate would have five months taken off of his sentence for every year of good behavior.

Floyd got into only minor scrapes while he was in the penitentiary. Once he lost sixty days good time for possessing narcotics. In 1927, he hit a guard when the guard yelled at him for moving too slowly in the morning. That stunt cost him another sixty days. He also stole potatoes to make whiskey, but the prison officials were never able to catch him at that.

Despite his relatively clean record of behavior while in prison, events on the outside assured that Floyd's time in the penitentiary would affect him for the rest of his life. Shortly before Floyd was scheduled to be released, his wife filed for divorce. Floyd did not contest the divorce, and he remained devoted to her. This might explain why Floyd went to Kansas City shortly after his release on March 7, 1929.

When he first reached Kansas City, Floyd planned to try to make an honest living. But he couldn't find a job, and then he was arrested for a crime he didn't commit, simply because he was an ex-convict. Floyd later told reporters that after he got out of the penitentiary he got arrested everywhere he went. "I decided I'd just as well get the goods as have the name," he said. In early 1930, Floyd was back in Oklahoma robbing banks.

Floyd quickly developed a style. He and his partners would steal a getaway car. They did not bother to wear masks, but did wear bullet-proof vests. They were also heavily armed with machine guns. Leaving one man in the driver's seat of the getaway car, Floyd and his gang would enter the bank shortly before noon. After collecting the cash, they would lock any customers and employees in the vault. Then they would speed off to their hideouts in the Cookson Hills of Oklahoma.

During the 1930s, the Great Depression made life extremely difficult for most Americans. Disillusioned with official leaders, many were sympathetic to gangsters. Floyd had many supporters among the common folk who lived in the Cookson Hills where he typically hid. Floyd gave generously to the poor in exchange for help and concealment. There are reports that one night he burglarized a grocery store, filled up a truck with things to eat, and drove around the hills distributing the food. Other people said that he tore up mortgages during his robberies to protect poor farmers who were in danger of losing their land.

By 1931, Floyd's methods had become a science. Fast cars and loyal supporters made him difficult to catch. By 1932, he had hit the big time. Newspapers compared him to Billy the Kid and Wild Bill Hickock. Policemen blamed him for robberies in far-off states, sometimes even multiple robberies that occurred at the same time. Bankers hated him as their insurance rates rose.

Even when taunting the authorities, Pretty Boy maintained his Robin Hood persona. In January 1932, the governor of Oklahoma offered a $1,000 reward for his capture. Floyd responded by sending a letter to the governor: "You will either withdraw that $1,000 reward at once or suffer the consequences—no kidding. I have robbed no one but the monied men."

His image allowed him to do some amazing things. Probably the best example was the robbery of the bank in Sallisaw, Oklahoma, where Floyd had grown up. Floyd and his gang approached the bank at about 11:30 in the morning. As they got out of their car, Floyd greeted friends at the barbershop, telling them to "lay off the telephone." Inside, he was courtesy itself. "It's a hold-up, all right," he told the victims, but then he added an aside to his accomplice: "Don't hurt 'em, Bird, they're friends of mine." Floyd and his accomplices made off safely, even though the chief of police was sitting just around the corner.

Throughout the winter of 1932 and 1933, the FBI placed more emphasis on catching gangsters. They sent petty criminals to infiltrate Floyd's gang, including one of his old cell mates from the Missouri State Penitentiary. Still, they were unable to bring Pretty Boy down.

It was only the horror of the Kansas City Massacre that allowed the authorities to gather the forces needed to catch Floyd. In the spring of 1933, a man named Frank Nash, who had escaped from Leavenworth, was captured in Hot Springs, Arkansas. Federal authorities put Nash on a train to Kansas City. Members of the underworld hired Floyd and his partner Adam Richetti to help free Nash as he was transferred from the train to a car for the ride back to Leavenworth. Nash and his escort got off the train and made it to the car. As they were getting settled, three men approached and opened fire. Unfortunately for Nash, Floyd and Richetti had never met him, and he was killed in the rain of bullets meant to free him.

The killings became known as the Kansas City Massacre. Afterwards, Congress passed laws strengthening the FBI. The new laws gave FBI agents the power to arrest suspects and carry weapons. They also increased the number of federal crimes, which meant the FBI became responsible for more investigations.

Floyd and Richetti became hunted men. The underworld bosses in Kansas City who had hired them would not help them escape for fear of getting caught themselves. Eventually, Floyd and Richetti made it to Buffalo, New York, where they managed to lay low for several months. Meanwhile, the FBI sent agents to watch Floyd's family and increased the reward for his capture. In September 1934, J. Edgar Hoover declared Floyd to be Public Enemy Number 1.

In October 1934, Floyd and Richetti left their hideout to visit family. On October 20, Floyd ran their car into a telephone pole in Ohio. Floyd and Richetti hid in the woods while their two companions sought help. While they waited, a local man encountered them and thought they were suspicious because they were so heavily armed. He reported what he had seen to the local police. When the police arrived, Floyd attempted to convince them that he and Richetti were just lost, but the police did not believe him, and shots were fired. Richetti surrendered but Floyd managed to escape into the woods. For two days, lawmen scoured the hills while Floyd eluded them, living on wild fruit.

Finally, Floyd approached a farmhouse and asked for a meal. The widow who lived there cooked him pork chops. Afterwards, Floyd asked the widow's brother for a ride to a nearby town. Although the man was suspicious of the armed stranger, he eventually agreed. As they pulled out of the driveway, however, two cars approached. The widow's brother ordered Floyd out of the car. The two approaching cars stopped, and police and FBI agents leaped out. Floyd dashed for the woods, and shots rang out. Floyd fell; he had been hit twice through the chest and once in the arm. The agents carried him to the shade of a nearby apple tree where he died fifteen minutes later.

Although Floyd never saw the inside of a prison after his short stint at the beginning of his career, the story of the Kansas City Massacre did return to the walls of the Missouri State Penitentiary. After his capture in October 1934, Adam Richetti stood trial for the killings. He was convicted and sentenced to death. On October 7, 1935, Floyd's partner met his end in the gas chamber at the Missouri State Penitentiary.

Early Efforts to Reform Prisoners

A boxing match is like a cowboy movie. There's got to be good guys and bad guys. And that's what people pay for—to see the bad guys get beat. —Sonny Liston

The penitentiary system was founded upon the theory that men could be changed. Reformers believed that with the right programs and training, men who had committed heinous crimes could become productive members of society. Around the turn of the twentieth century, it began to become apparent that prisoners needed more than solitary contemplation and hard work if they were to complete the transformation reformers had in mind. In the first half of the twentieth century, the Missouri State Penitentiary took the first faltering steps towards becoming a modern correctional system.

In the 1800s, when reformers focused on contemplation as a means of instilling remorse in the convict, the primary provision for reform was the prison library. However, in Missouri, even this meager provision was given short shrift. The library was under the charge of the part-time chaplain and was continually underfunded. In the 1860s, only $25 per year was provided for maintaining the library. In 1864, the prison inspectors declared in their annual report to the Missouri senate that the amount was "entirely too small an amount to supply the demand for new reading material by the convicts. It is scarcely enough to furnish the library with any one series of standard works upon history, romance or science." With this small budget, the prison library could not perform its function of reforming the convicts.

Even if the prison library had been adequately funded, there was another major problem with relying on it as the primary means of educating the convicts: many of the prisoners could not read. Teaching inmates who wished to learn to read became the responsibility of the part-time chaplain because there was no money to hire teachers. Prison officials asked almost every year that the chaplain be given a salary large enough to permit him to devote his full time to the penitentiary, but for decades, the legislature failed to act.

The second problem with relying on leisure-time reading as an agent of reform had to do with the cells where the prisoners lived. Until 1871, the prisoners were not allowed candles or other lighting for fear of fire. Without light to read, more books would have served little purpose.

The lack of funding also affected the condition of the library. Without money, mutilated or worn books were usually not replaced. Furthermore, there was no direction or plan used in purchasing volumes. Each chaplain bought items he thought to be beneficial, and subsequent chaplains frequently complained about the books purchased by those who came before.

As Missouri struggled through the years after the Civil War, the inspectors realized that the administrators' focus on profit combined with the inadequacies of the prison library made true reform exceedingly difficult. In their 1873 report to the legislature, the Missouri Board of Guardians suggested hiring a full-time instructor to teach illiterate prisoners to read. In support, they noted, "Surely the State should not hesitate, while enjoying the benefits of their penal labor to confer upon them a boon so cheaply purchased and so eagerly sought." Still, the chaplains' reports in the 1880s show that the legislature neither hired a teacher nor appropriated sufficient funds for a full-time chaplain. A full-time chaplain was not hired until 1893.

As the failures of the prison library as an agent of reform began to show, another popular theory developed. Progressive thinkers began to think that music would help reform prisoners. In 1899, the penitentiary chaplain started a convict orchestra. One reporter who heard the orchestra play stated, "A good song is better than a bad sermon," and praised music as an agent of reform because it could touch the needs of diverse groups of prisoners. Over the years, many different musical groups were organized among the convicts. In addition to the orchestra, several bands were organized. The groups played for their fellow inmates, on the radio, and at official state functions.

One inmate was even able to turn his musical experiences at the prison into a professional musical career. In 1923, Harry Milton Snodgrass was sentenced to three years in the Missouri State Penitentiary for armed robbery. Shortly after his arrival, his talent for the piano was noticed and he was assigned to play with the orchestra. Later, the orchestra began to play for the local radio station. The announcer for Jefferson City's local radio station called Snodgrass "King of the Ivories," and his popularity spawned efforts for his release. In January 1925, Governor Sam Baker commuted Snodgrass's sentence. After his release, Snodgrass had several records released on the Brunswick label.

The effort needed to obtain an early release for Snodgrass was symptomatic of early attempts to inspire prisoners to good behavior through promises of early release. When the penitentiary first opened, executive clemency was the only possibility for early release. Officials soon began requesting a law allowing the reduction of an inmate's sentence based on good conduct while imprisoned. As this provision had no out-of-pocket cost, the legislature adopted it in December 1865. The first good-time law provided that a prisoner would be released after he had completed three-fourths of his sentence, so long as his conduct while in prison was good. However, release under this law still required review by the governor.

This system became impractical as the prison population soared in the early 1920s. The governor could not carefully review all the petitions he received, and prisoners complained that politics rather than reform governed the decisions. In 1918, a merit system was developed to help determine when paroles should be granted and when prisoners should be allowed certain privileges. In 1937, Governor

Lloyd Stark signed into law a bill that created a separate board of probation and parole.

Around that time, attitudes toward dealing with prisoners became more scientific. After 1937, when inmates entered the system they were classified based on their age and criminal history. The goal was to separate the incorrigibles from the young men who could be reformed. However, the facilities had been built with a different theory in mind, and segregating the prisoners for different treatment and work assignments was almost impossible. A few young men could be diverted to the reformatories at Boonville and Algoa, but the majority of men were confined in the main penitentiary, and a true treatment system remained a goal rather than a reality.

The first real school at the Missouri State Penitentiary opened on January 2, 1940. The school operated using inmate teachers and donated school books. It was so popular that the student body quadrupled in the first year. But capacity and reforms never kept up with the growing inmate population. Throughout the fifties, the school proceeded in fits and starts.

During this time, the primary reformatory efforts remained the province of the chaplains. In addition to sponsoring musical groups, the Protestant chaplain continued to expand the library, and the Catholic chaplain became responsible for a recreation program. In 1933, the recreation program, supported by profits from the inmate canteen, provided opportunities for inmates to participate in softball, boxing, and football. By 1949, the boxing club was putting on monthly exhibitions throughout the summer, and it "always" had "an enthusiastic following," officials reported. Officials had come to believe that athletics could benefit prisoners as much as hard work because sports functioned "as an outlet for pent up energies," and "encourages clean sportsmanship."

For some inmates, like Sonny Liston, the athletic program worked famously. Liston was the twelfth of seventeen children who grew up in a poor, abusive family. He worked odd jobs in St. Louis until he fell in with a rough crowd and was eventually convicted of first-degree robbery and theft. He arrived at the penitentiary in June 1950.

Liston quickly adapted to life behind the walls. He worked in the laundry, felt no need to complain about the food, and participated in the boxing program. In the boxing ring, Liston was able to turn his tough upbringing into a virtue. The chaplain and athletic director at the time, Reverend Edward Schlattman, saw Liston's potential and began the work of turning Liston into a professional prizefighter. As historian Gary Kremer reported in his book *Heartland History*, Liston's trainer, a fellow inmate, once said that Liston "was the real thing right away. You'd show him a punch or a technique and by the end of the day he had it down. But poor, poor Sonny. He could fight and that was it. He had the mind of an eleven-year-old, an overgrown kid. He could be the sweetest guy in the world, and then he'd just snap, go off. But there's no denying it—he could hit like a mule. Pretty soon there was no one left inside who would get in the ring with him."

Father Schlattman arranged for a newspaper reporter to watch Liston box. The reporter was so impressed that he joined the priest

Sonny Liston lines up a punch in a bout against another inmate boxer. In 1961, as Floyd Patterson prepared to meet Sonny Liston to defend his title as the heavyweight champion of the world, President Kennedy told Patterson "You've GOT to beat this guy" because Liston was seen as too mean. Courtesy of Missouri State Archives.

in a campaign to secure a parole for Liston. Liston was released in 1952, and turned pro in 1953. In 1962, he squared off against the world heavyweight champion, Floyd Patterson, and knocked Patterson out in just two minutes and six seconds. Liston held the title until he was defeated by Muhammad Ali in 1964. Liston's story was so inspiring that a mural of him in fighting stance can still be seen on the decaying prison walls.

Still, for many prisoners, these informal attempts at training and rehabilitation were not sufficient. More organization was necessary. On June 30, 1946, the penitentiary, along with five other institutions, was turned over to the newly created Department of Corrections. The Department of Corrections represented the final shift from the original theory of the penitentiary as a place of hard work and contemplation to a newer theory of the penitentiary as a place for treatment and rehabilitation. "Correctional work necessitates a program of education and training that is thorough and adapted to the practical needs of prisoners and prison conditions," officials said. Under the direction of the Department of Correction, the penitentiary became one part in a massive system designed to treat offenders rather than to punish them. The department had subdivisions devoted to education, classification, industries, and inmate health.

Even though reformers recognized the need for these programs and began to set them up, politicians were still unwilling to spend the sums needed to effect true change. During the middle part of the twentieth century, the system limped toward reform. And while the legislature delayed, life at the penitentiary, hard and sometimes violent, went on.

12:01 a.m.

The Death Penalty at the Missouri State Penitentiary

The actual act of execution I don't think is cruel and unusual. It's what leads up to it. —A. J. Bannister, death row inmate, quoted in Stephen Trombley, *The Execution Protocol*

Along with early twentieth-century reforms came a darker aspect of the criminal justice system. As society became more settled and centralized, public hangings became a thing of the past, but the need to punish violent criminals did not. The death penalty came to the Missouri State Penitentiary.

The death sentence has never been a penalty that Missouri citizens have imposed lightly. Before 1900, all first-degree murders were punishable by death, but instead of condemning men to hang, juries would find the defendant guilty of the lesser crime of second-degree murder. Second-degree murder carried a penalty of life in prison, so the condemned man's life was spared. In 1917, the Missouri legislature even abolished the death penalty, although the legislators quickly changed their minds and reinstated it in 1919.

Around this time, a new abhorrence to the death penalty developed because of the way executions were conducted during the late nineteenth and early twentieth centuries. By the late 1800s, hangings had become a public spectacle, and this practice did not sit well with Victorian-era sensibilities.

Victorians found it difficult to accept the theories of criminal justice and the corresponding practices that had been a part of life in the American colonies and the early years of the nation. In colonial times, criminals were seen not as individuals to be reformed but as sinners to be punished and thus made a warning for the faithful. Punishments tended to be public so that the wrongdoer could be made into an example. The most common punishments were fines for the wealthy, and whipping, mutilation, shaming, the stocks, or banishment for the less well-to-do. These practices continued into the early republic even as the ideas of the Enlightenment began to shift the focus of penological theory. Prisons, like the one in Missouri, took the place of the stocks and the whipping post. Unfortunately, the gallows was a colonial tradition that was retained.

In Missouri throughout the 1800s, executions were conducted in the county that pronounced sentence. The condemned awaited his fate in the county jail, and executions typically took place within a year of the verdict. The executions were open to the public, and the condemned frequently gave a final speech in a kind of macabre morality play. Afterwards, there was a ritual viewing of the body, and the hangman frequently cut the noose into pieces to sell as souvenirs.

During the early 1900s, officials began to adjust the time of hangings to minimize crowds, but the "carnival atmosphere" continued. Missouri's last hanging occurred in 1937 in Kennett. A ten-foot-high plank enclosure had been built around the scaffold and tickets were required to attend, but that did not decrease the interest in the event. The execution was scheduled for eight in the morning. As the time approached, the streets surrounding the Dunklin County Jail were filled with spectators. Boys climbed up to the roofs of surrounding buildings for a glimpse of the scaffold. Shortly after 8 a.m., the trap door was sprung, and Fred Adams died for his role in the killing of night marshal Clarence Green.

One attending legislator was so affected by the atmosphere surrounding the execution that when he returned to Jefferson City the next year, he introduced a bill to move all executions to the penitentiary. Prison officials objected, arguing that the shift would harm prisoner morale and possibly lead to riots. But the political pressure was high; at the time of the bill, the only other states that still executed men in the county in which they had been convicted were Kansas, Louisiana, and Mississippi. On June 4, 1937, Missouri governor Lloyd Stark signed into law a bill mandating that all prisoners condemned to death be executed by lethal gas at the penitentiary in Jefferson City.

After the passage of the execution bill, Missouri's first death row was established in a basement of one of the cell blocks at the prison. There, prisoners experienced some of the worst conditions imaginable. They were completely separated from the other prisoners. The cells had no natural light and were subject to flooding. The death-row inmates were only allowed to leave their cells for forty-five minutes of exercise three times a week. Until a lawsuit forced the prison

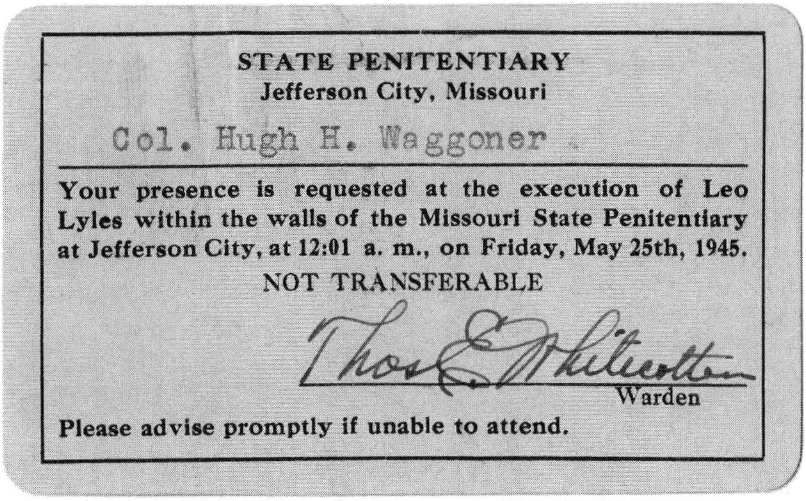

STATE PENITENTIARY
Jefferson City, Missouri

Col. Hugh H. Waggoner

Your presence is requested at the execution of Leo Lyles within the walls of the Missouri State Penitentiary at Jefferson City, at 12:01 a. m., on Friday, May 25th, 1945.

NOT TRANSFERABLE

Warden

Please advise promptly if unable to attend.

After the law was changed to require that all executions in Missouri take place at the Missouri State Penitentiary, attendance at an execution was by invitation only. This was another measure taken to help reduce the spectacle of executions. Attendees were provided with a card like the one pictured above. Courtesy of Missouri State Archives.

to adopt new procedures in 1987, the prisoners only received two meals a day. In these dungeons, men awaited their fate.

The chemical used in the Missouri gas chamber was cyanide gas. To create the gas, cyanide tablets were dropped into a bucket of sulfuric acid. The chemical reaction between the two ingredients released the poisonous gas. Once the gas was released, the victim often tried to hold his breath to delay the moment of death. Eventually, however, the victim breathed in the gas, which paralyzed the lungs and heart. The result was not pleasant to watch. In the words of Stephen Trombley, who wrote *The Execution Protocol: Inside America's Capital Punishment Industry*, "The victim struggles vainly for breath, eyes popping, tongue hanging thick and swollen from a drooling mouth. His face turns purple."

Because the gas permeates the air, special precautions had to be taken when performing an execution by lethal gas. First, the gas had to be contained during the execution. In Missouri, the inmates built what became known as the "death house."

The structure of the death house reflects its serious purpose. The building is made of stone and shaped like a cross. White crosses are painted on the sidewalk leading to the entrance. The building only has space for a few observers, and there are no windows to tempt the curious. Mug shots of each victim are displayed—a warning to others to avoid a life of crime.

But cyanide gas is extremely volatile, and a simple structure is not enough to protect the executioners from the lethal effect of the gas. Inside the death house, a special chamber was built by Eaton Metal Products, a company headquartered in Denver, Colorado, that specialized in making large metal containers such as silos and storage tanks. Special seals were placed on the doors to ensure that the gas would not escape. The circular seals gave the chamber the feel of a submarine or space ship.

After an execution, the gas was vented into the atmosphere for twenty minutes before it was safe for prison employees to enter the chamber and remove the body. The entire chamber then had to be sprayed with ammonia to neutralize the gas. During the execution, the victim's body and clothes would become saturated with the gas, so they also had to be treated. The victim's body was cleaned with ammonia, and the clothes the victim had worn during the execution were destroyed.

The first execution by lethal gas to take place at the Missouri State Penitentiary was actually a double execution; John Brown and William Wright were put to death in the gas chamber at 6:21 a.m. on March 4, 1938. Brown had killed an off-duty police officer during an attempted robbery. Wright had been convicted in 1933 for shooting a Kansas City druggist named J. T. McCampbell. While the execution was held in the early morning like county hangings, only a select group of people were allowed to view the event.

After that execution, officials changed execution times to 12:01 a.m. This reflected the realization that an execution conducted in the seclusion of the penitentiary was much different than one conducted in public. It was the final break with the colonial tradition. The time was chosen because death warrants specify a date but not a time. Consequently, if there were a malfunction or a delay, there would be time to remedy it before the death warrant expired. The timing was also beneficial because it ensured that the execution would occur at a time when most other prisoners would be asleep.

To further separate the condemned from the ordinary flow of prison life, the death house at the penitentiary contained a single cell where the condemned would spend his final days. Depending on security considerations and the prisoner's wishes, the prisoner might spend up to a week in this cell. He was monitored around the clock but was allowed unlimited access to the prison canteen to buy snacks and other items and was allowed to have his friends and family members with him throughout most of the day.

The condemned man was not the only one whose daily routine was affected by the pending execution. Officials and other prisoners also developed rituals and procedures for the night before an execution. Officials secured all of the inmates at the penitentiary in their cells and sometimes played videos to keep the inmates' minds off the execution. By the 1990s, these videos were usually sexually explicit.

Some death-row inmates thought this was disrespectful and boycotted the videos. They began a separate tradition of "flicking their light switches on and off" at the time of the execution.

In total, forty-two executions were carried out at the penitentiary, most of them during the 1930s and 1940s. Only two prisoners were executed during the 1960s. The declining number of executions in Missouri reflected the attitude toward the death penalty in society at large. During the 1960s, Justice Warren Burger led the U.S. Supreme Court in greatly expanding the rights of the criminal accused with such landmark cases as *Miranda v. Arizona*, which required that every criminal suspect be warned that he had a right to remain silent when questioned by police. By the late 1960s and early 1970s, many states had in place a moratorium on the death penalty. The practice became universal after the U.S. Supreme Court case of *Furman v. Georgia*, which was decided in 1972. In that case, the Supreme Court held that while the death penalty did not violate the constitution's prohibition against cruel and unusual punishment, the current implementation did because it resulted in "arbitrary and capricious" application. Hundreds of death sentences were affected by this decision, and many states, including Missouri, began the work of writing new death penalty statutes that complied with the dictates of the Supreme Court.

Missouri enacted its new death penalty statute in 1977, and the law became effective on May 26, 1977. The first person to be executed under the new regulation was George "Tiny" Mercer. Mercer had been convicted of a brutal rape and murder. During his birthday celebration, Mercer's friends lured waitress Karen Keeten to their party. Mercer produced a shotgun and forced Keeter to have sex with him and with his friends. Afterwards, they killed her in an attempt to hide their culpability. In the court document denying Mercer's appeal, the judges reported that Mercer had confessed without remorse, mentioning to a cellmate that he wished he had killed the victim of another crime he had committed just as he had killed Keeter.

But life on death row changed Mercer. He took a new interest in religion, and he decorated his cell with religious items. Although many inmates turn to religion, the warden at the time of Mercer's execution, Bill Armontrout, later stated that he believed Mercer's conversion was genuine.

During his time in prison, Mercer made other improvements in his life. He married a girl from Jefferson City named Christy who visited him almost every afternoon. He spent time lifting weights and developed friendships with both guards and inmates. In an interview with Stephen Trombly, A. J. Bannister, the inmate in the cell next to Mercer's, recalled, "Tiny was well liked by the guards at [the prison] too, and they were visibly troubled by his pending execution."

Because Missouri had not executed a man in several decades, many preparations were needed. Missouri officials contacted a well-known designer of execution equipment, Fred Leuchter, to inspect Missouri's gas chamber. Leuchter said the chamber was likely to leak and gave prices for creating a new gas chamber and for building a lethal injection machine. A new gas chamber would cost the state $300,000, while a lethal injection machine would cost $30,000. Missouri officials chose the latter, but the statute had to be amended to allow lethal injection as a method of execution.

The new statute specified lethal injection as the manner of execution, and Fred Leuchter was employed to build a machine to administer the lethal injection. The lethal injunction is a combination of three drugs and requires precise timing. The goal of Leuchter's machine was to administer the drugs with a minimum of discomfort and chance for error.

Leuchter based his design on procedures used to euthanize animals. The first drug is sodium pentothal, which causes the victim to lose consciousness. Then pancuronium bromide and potassium chloride are injected to stop the heart and lungs. The drugs are administered precisely one minute apart, and the victim dies approximately two minutes after the last drug is injected. On the night of the execution, the victim is given a sedative and an IV is set up. The IV is connected to Leuchter's machine, which requires two operators. The operators begin the sequence, and then the machine automatically depresses the plungers at the right times. A backup allows the operators to depress the plungers manually if there is a malfunction. A technician monitors the victim's breathing and heart rate. A

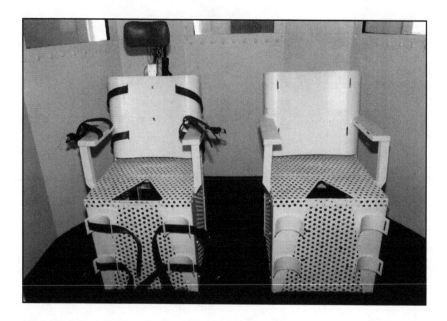

Each chair inside the gas chamber had holes in the seat so that material from the bowel and bladder expelled during death would not pool underneath the victim's body. These chairs were removed to make way for a hospital gurney when the legislature mandated that execution should take place by lethal injection. Courtesy of Missouri State Archives.

doctor is on hand to declare the time of death. This procedure creates a hospital-like atmosphere that supporters argued was more humane. Governor John Ashcroft signed the law authorizing lethal injection as a method of execution, and it became effective on August 13, 1988.

The injection machine was not the only preparation for Mercer's execution at the penitentiary. Because the penitentiary was located within Jefferson City and officials feared a protest, security was a major concern. Water patrol, the highway patrol, and the capital police assisted the guards in patrolling the area. The guards in the towers on the prison's walls were armed with shotguns.

As it turned out, the precautions were unnecessary. On the night of the execution, only about a hundred protestors stood outside the prison. They stood silently, holding candles and carrying signs. Mercer had his last meal, and his wife was allowed to stay with him until he went into the death chamber.

At 11:00 p.m., the doctor arrived. Because Mercer had used drugs heavily in the past, the doctor had to perform what was called an IV cutdown to reach the vein. This procedure involved making an incision to reveal the vein and then inserting the needle directly into the vein. After the IV was placed, Mercer was put on a hospital gurney and wheeled into the death chamber. As the death warrant was read, he mouthed "I love you" to his wife. Mercer died quietly at 12:09 a.m.

Mercer was the last man executed at the Missouri State Penitentiary. After that, death row was moved to the newly built Potosi Correctional Center in Washington County. Executions would take place there as well. Potosi was in a rural area, which would make it easier to take the necessary security precautions. The prison there was also populated exclusively by prisoners who were either under sentence of death or serving life without parole. Consequently, there was no need to separate the death row inmates from the general population, and Missouri's death row inmates received a drastic improvement in the conditions of their confinement.

Moving death row to Potosi was part of the surge in prison building that drove Missouri away from the old penitentiary system. To understand this trend, it is necessary to go back to the 1950s, an era when lack of funding meant that hard work and poor conditions were still the pillars of the penitentiary's reform agenda.

Riot!

The State of Missouri is now paying a terrific price for its adherence to the philosophy that men can be locked up and then forgotten. —Missouri State Penal Institutions Survey Committee, Report and Recommendations

In the 1920s and 1930s, tensions in prisons across the country began to build. The 1930s saw a dramatic rise in the prison population that one Missouri warden blamed on fast cars, short skirts, and moonshine. When this population increase was combined with the phasing out of the contract labor system in response to pressures from organized labor, an explosive situation resulted. There were more inmates confined in the prison, and because of the demise of the contract labor system, they had increasingly fewer productive activities to occupy their time. In Missouri, those tensions came to a head in September 1954. The Missouri riot was not the first of the prison riots across the nation, but many observers thought that it was the one that authorities had handled most appropriately. The riot brought national attention to Missouri's correctional system and changed the penitentiary's relationship with Jefferson City forever.

Although officials later denied seeing any warning signs, they were not totally unprepared for the outbreak of violence. During the summer of 1954, Missouri governor Phil Donnelly gathered with highway patrol officials to watch a video that had been made about a prison riot that had occurred in Michigan in 1952. Donnelly told the patrolmen, "If there is ever a riot in Missouri, I want you all to stop it. Don't ask me what to do. You stop it."

In the late afternoon of September 22, 1954, a routine problem quickly got out of hand. Inmate Don DeLapp was being held in the maximum security building known as "E Hall," which was reserved for those inmates who were considered incorrigible. He broke the faucet in his cell, and the guard on duty brought in a plumber to fix it. After the faucet had been repaired, DeLapp complained that his bedding was wet, and it was replaced. A third time, DeLapp called for the guard's attention. Although the guards were under strict orders not to open a cell in E Hall unless at least two guards were present, the guard returned alone to DeLapp's cell. This time, when the guard opened the door to the cell, DeLapp shoved the door back, knocking the guard off balance. DeLapp grabbed the guard's keys, and fifteen hours of mayhem began.

DeLapp ran through E Hall releasing prisoners. They moved throughout the prison, opening doors and lighting fires. "Come on out they are having a riot!" the inmates yelled, inviting their fellows. One inmate obtained gas and set the pants shop on fire because he "was just mad at the pants shop." It took almost an hour for officials to begin to respond. During that time, "there was a building fury," one observer later remembered when questioned by historian Gary Kremer.

Just before six that evening, the captain of the local highway patrol troop, Maurice Parker, was sitting down to dinner when the phone rang. The superintendent of the highway patrol, Colonel Hugh Waggoner, was on the line. After a hurried conversation, Parker threw on his uniform and rushed to the office where he ordered his entire troop out to the prison. When Parker told Waggoner that his troop was on the way, Waggoner replied, "Hell, bring them all in."

Fires burning uncontrolled on the night of September 22, 1954. Courtesy of Missouri State Archives.

Warden Ralph Edison later recalled that when he arrived at the prison there were more highway patrolmen on the grounds than he had ever seen. He turned the situation over to the highway patrol, and troopers mounted the watchtowers with orders to shoot any convict that made it to the walls.

Troopers poured in from across the state, some driving so fast they destroyed the engines in their patrol cars and had to flag down other troopers to give them a lift. As the cars approached Jefferson City, they formed convoys. Local police departments cleared the roads so the troopers could continue on their way without delay. "There were times when there were ten, fifteen patrol cars, one right behind the other—at a high rate of speed," one observer later recalled. The troopers made it to Jefferson City in record time. A patrolman from the Kansas City area claimed to have made the 150-mile trip in just over an hour.

Members of the highway patrol gather with prison administrators to help bring the rioting prisoners under control. Many historians believe that the lightning fast reaction of the highway patrol during the 1954 Riot gave the patrol the public support they needed to become a respected state-wide law enforcement agency as opposed to an agency devoted to traffic problems. Courtesy of Missouri State Archives.

The troopers arrived at a scene out of Dante's *Inferno*. The prisoners were entirely out of control. A reporter from the *Jefferson City Post-Tribune* who happened to be on the scene said that men were "tearing up anything they could get their hands on and were burning everything that would burn." Inmates shouted and hurled bricks; smoke whirled through the darkness. Over it all, the prison escape siren wailed.

At approximately 7:20 p.m., the inmates charged toward the office of the deputy warden. The trooper manning the patrol's only Thompson submachine gun ordered the inmates back, but they kept coming, and the trooper opened fire, joined by several other troopers with shotguns. A number of inmates were wounded, and the rest fled back to the cellblocks for cover. About a half an hour later, troopers worked the yard in wedges to begin restoring order.

By 8:00 p.m., with the inmates in control of two cellblocks and the highway patrol in control of the walls and the yard, an uneasy truce settled. Several guards and the prison teacher were still unaccounted for. The fires raged, uncontrolled; the license plate factory, where many chemicals and metals were stored, eventually "burst into a galaxy of colors amid billowing black and white smoke."

At 9:00 p.m., the inmates presented a list of demands, including that they be allowed to speak with the press. Governor Donnelly entered the prison yard to talk with the inmate representative, and a reporter from the *Jefferson City Post-Tribune* witnessed the conversation. The reporter explained that the governor told the inmate, "We're not going to negotiate with anybody . . . until we get those guards out of there and until everyone is back in their cells."

"No deal," came the response. "They're not going to do that."

Governor Donnelly held the line, saying, "If you harm the hair on the head of one of those guards, we will kill the whole bunch."

"It's going to be rough, governor," the inmate replied.

After that terse exchange, things settled down for the night. Gordon Slovut, a reporter who spent the night in the riot-torn prison, provided an intimate account of the night for the *Jefferson City Post-Tribune*. In the administrative offices of the prison, patrolmen and prison officials made plans to retake the resisting cellblocks as soon as the sun came up. Phones rang and newsmen milled about. Periodically during the early morning hours, inmates would emerge cautiously from the cellblock, some to surrender, others to attempt to negotiate.

One of those to emerge was inmate Jack Noble. He came to the door of B Hall and called for a stretcher. When it was brought, one of the missing guards, Clarence Dietzel, was carried out, limp and contorted. He had been beaten and had suffered a wound to his leg. Later, Dietzel recounted a night of horror. First, the inmates "took him to the top tier of cells in B Hall and threatened to push him off if no concessions were made." Later he was threatened with a butcher knife. The inmate with the knife said he never had killed a prison guard and speculated about how exciting that would be.

Another guard was luckier. He was found by a group of friendly inmates, and one of them loaned the guard his convict shirt and cap. The others then escorted him to the prison entrance. By morning, all of the guards who had been unaccounted for were safely outside the walls.

Early the next morning, the highway patrol troopers were organized into two squads of seventeen men each, one under the command of Lieutenant Willie Barton and the other under the command

Clarence Deitzel, pictured here on the stretcher shortly after he was released by the rioting prisoners, spent several hours as a hostage during the 1954 Riot. His captors threatened to kill him just so they could see what it would feel like to kill a guard. Courtesy of Missouri State Archives.

of Lieutenant H. D. Brigham. The troopers under Brigham were to subdue the cellblock known as B Hall while Barton and his men were to subdue C Hall. After being given instructions, the troopers marched into the prison guns at the ready. "We mean business," they shouted, and ordered the convicts back into the cells.

All went quietly in B Hall, but in C Hall, the inmates shouted insults at the armed troopers. One inmate had stashed several items on an upper tier to throw down at any one who tried to mount the steps to reach him. As the inmate threatened to throw down a typewriter, one of the troopers fired. The inmate was struck in the face and fell backwards, dead. The hall fell silent, and the riot was over.

At the end of the riot, many prisoners were hustled into random cells, just to regain control. The morning was spent searching prisoners for weapons and getting them back into their proper cells. As the highway patrol and the National Guard took care of this task, administrators surveyed the damage, which was extensive.

Four inmates had been killed in the riot. During the cleanup, the most horrific sight encountered by the crews was the body of an inmate named Walter Lee Donnell. In 1953, Donnell had turned state's witness and had testified against four other men who had participated with him in a holdup. Donnell knew the dangers of being a "snitch." While still in the St. Louis jail, he had been stabbed. In an article after the riot, the *Jefferson City Post-Tribune* reported that Donnell had "begged authorities not to send him to the state prison because he was afraid of reprisal."

When Donnell had finally arrived at the prison, he was kept segregated from the other prisoners for his own safety. But that was not enough to save him during the riot. A small group of convicts led by Rollie Lassiter, one of the men Donnell had betrayed, smashed into Donnell's cell with sledge hammers. They stabbed Donnell numerous times, reminding him repeatedly of the role he had played in getting his companions convicted. When it became apparent that Donnell could not take any more abuse, his tormentors cut out his tongue and slashed his throat. Then, for good measure, they beat his head with a sledge hammer.

Riot ringleaders appear to face charges in Cole County Circuit Court. Courtesy of Missouri State Archives.

Three other inmates were killed during the riot. One was another snitch, killed by the rioting prisoners, and two were killed by patrol gunfire. Thirty were injured, many seriously.

The damage to the prison facilities was also extensive. Because the fire department was unable to enter the prison during the riot, the fires became so fierce that they had to be allowed to simply burn themselves out. Several factories were completely ruined, and in others not a window remained unbroken. The prisoners were quickly put to work cleaning up the mess, but even with inmate labor to help defray the cost, some officials estimated that the riot had caused as much as $5 million in damage.

In the end, seven men were indicted for the murder of Donnell, and two commissions were appointed to study the causes of the riot. These commissions, one appointed by the governor and the other by the legislature, noted many deficiencies in Missouri's handling of prisoners. The suggestions in their reports echoed complaints that had been heard for years, but the publicity surrounding the riot created the momentum needed to begin to bring real reform to the Missouri State Penitentiary.

Riot Aftermath

Our job is to salvage broken lives. —Fred T. Wilkinson, *The Realities of Crime and Punishment*

As the embers of the riot fires cooled, a question remained in the minds of many citizens: what was the cause of so much violence? Interviews with inmates and two official inquiries provided a variety of answers, all of which were based at least in part on the overcrowded conditions and the old, crumbling facilities. The legislature was slow to take the action that was needed. Violence continued throughout the next decade until at last Missouri sought outside help.

On September 23, 1954, the day after the riot, the headlines in Jefferson City's leading newspaper, the *Jefferson City Post-Tribune,* had announced "Governor Promises Shakedown of Riot-Torn Prison." A hundred St. Louis policemen helped the penitentiary guards conduct a methodical search of the entire prison. As historian Mark Schrieber reported in his book *Somewhere in Time: 170 Years of Missouri Corrections,* "The search revealed an enormous arsenal of weaponry: sledgehammers, axe handles, screwdrivers, scissors, files and pieces of heavy machinery filed down to sharp deadly points."

The first dribbles of information about the cause of the riot came from the guards and others who had been unlucky enough to have been held hostage during the riot. The *Jefferson City Post-Tribune* reported that Guard Clarence Dietzel "said his captors told him the riot was in protest against 'poor food' and 'stool pigeons.'" Stool pigeons were prisoners who reported violations of the prison rules to the guards and often received special treatment in exchange for the information they provided. This rankled the prisoners who were punished for violations of the rules.

Poor food made life miserable even if a prisoner did not misbehave. Another guard who had been held hostage learned from the inmates that the watermelon at dinner the night before had been "uneatable." When the reporters were finally able to talk to the inmates themselves, the complaints were even more colorful. One inmate said they had to pay if they wanted such luxuries as milk, while another complained that the penitentiary kitchen served spaghetti raw.

Prisoners also blasted the parole board. Just prior to the riot, Governor Phil Donnelly had appointed three former highway patrol members to the parole board. "They're coppers," an inmate complained to a reporter from the *Jefferson City Post-Tribune*, "And it's coppers who put us in here." Prisoners wanted an investigation by outside authorities.

Surprisingly, the inmates were not the only ones to blame the riot on poor management. Harold Butterfield, a man running for state auditor, blamed the governor for failing to fire the director of the Department of Corrections, telling the *St. Louis Globe-Democrat* in September that the riot was the "tragic result of government by cronies." The governor and the legislature both ordered separate official inquiries.

While the investigators took testimony, tensions continued to simmer in the prison. In late October there was more violence at the penitentiary. On the 22nd, there was an incident in the dining hall. Inmates, still angry about the poor quality of the food, protested. The angry men broke plates and threw their food at the guards. On the 25th, the inmates would not go to lunch. Again the highway patrol was called to the penitentiary. The inmates ate that night at gun-point, and there is no record of complaints about that meal.

The first official report about the causes of the riot to be complet-ed was the one ordered by the governor. The governor's committee was made up of experts from across the nation. It released its report, titled the Report and Recommendations of the Missouri State Penal Institutions Survey, in December 1954. The ninety-two-page docu-ment described the conditions at the penitentiary and issued recom-mendations for reform. Committee members found deficiencies in every area they examined.

At least two of the problems needing major improvement were the direct result of the legislature's failure to appropriate sufficient mon-ey to run the penitentiary. The first issue the committee addressed was the condition of the physical facilities—the cellblocks, factories, and other buildings. The penitentiary structures sprawled over the forty-two-acre campus in a haphazard way. Most were old and diffi-cult to maintain. After years without enough money for repairs, pris-oners found living and working in the buildings intolerable.

Personnel and administration were also problems that could be directly traced to lack of funding. Few if any of the guards had any training, and there was no clear chain of command. For these prob-lems, the committee recommended the creation of a separate De-partment of Corrections with a planning staff and training for all new employees. The committee also recommended pay raises for the guards and more funding for prison operations.

Another set of problems had been created by old-fashioned peni-tentiary system thinking about how to reform convicts. In this area, the report first criticized the disciplining of prisoners. Although whippings were a thing of the past, punishment could still be harsh. For the most part, prisoners were punished with loss of privileges. In extreme cases, however, men would be confined to punishment cells. These cells were approximately eight by four feet and lacked both toi-let facilities and light. No bedding was provided to the unfortunate prisoners sent there. What's more, the punishment was imposed in an arbitrary manner. The committee recommended a rule book for inmates and a more systematic method for imposing punishment.

The report relied heavily on the *Manual of Correctional Standards* by the American Prison Association. One of the major developments explained in the *Manual* was the idea of classification. According to the *Manual*, "CLASSIFICATION is the term used to designate the organized procedure by which diagnosis, treatment planning, and the execution of the treatment program is coordinated on the individual case." Although a classification department had been created at the penitentiary in the 1940s, by the time of the riot, the legislature had only provided sufficient funds to hire four people in that department. Because of the small size of the staff, the function of the classification department was limited to assigning new inmates to their jobs in the institution. The report noted that "the importance of classification in institutional operation is being increasingly recognized . . . no progressively operated institution can function satisfactorily without a well organized personnel and procedure." The report discussed other programs that professional prison administrators now deemed essential for reform including vocational training, health care, and education.

Classification was a manifestation of a new trend in expert thinking about how to handle criminals. Under this theory, criminals were seen not as sinners to be reformed but as patients to be healed. The 1954 riot, many believed, was a symptom of Missouri's failure to recognize that the older penitentiary system had not worked. Unfortunately for legislators who liked to promise that they were keeping costs low, these new ideas also required increases in spending on Missouri's correctional system.

The committee's discussion of the problems with the parole board also reflected a concern with the goal of rehabilitation as achieved through treatment. The report noted that, as the inmates had told the reporters, the parole board consisted entirely of former members of the highway patrol. Inmates received their first parole hearing one year into their sentence, but after that, the system was haphazard. Getting a case before the parole board often required intercession from sources outside the correctional system. The report stated mildly, "The lack of some indication as to when there is likelihood of parole consideration after the initial meeting with the parole board imposes a condition which is a source of serious discontent among inmates." The prisoners had been more forceful in their assessment. During the riot, one inmate had yelled that the riot would not have happened if there had been a real parole board.

The second problem with the parole system was that almost no provision was made to help former convicts adjust to life outside the walls. Again, the committee referred to standards set by the American Prison Association that discussed the success of the parolee in terms borrowed from the medical profession, in which the ideas of planning and treatment replaced the ideas of punishment and repentance. The members of the governor's committee suggested prerelease training at an intermediate custody level. This suggestion ultimately prompted the establishment of halfway houses such as the Kay Cee Honor Center in Kansas City.

The report of the committee commissioned by the legislature appeared during the spring of 1955. It also emphasized rehabilitation rather than punishment. For the most part, the members of the legislative committee unabashedly echoed the findings and recommendations of the governor's committee. It differed in one important respect, however; the legislative committee suggested long-term study of the question of whether an additional penal facility should be built, recommending the creation of a permanent Joint Committee on Correctional Institutions that would provide the legislature with the information it needed to oversee the state's penal institutions and properly assess the need for additional institutions.

In July 1955, the director of the Department of Corrections, Thomas Whitecotton, resigned. The governor conducted a nationwide search for a qualified individual. James D. Carter, a former marine, was appointed on July 25, 1955. Carter was optimistic about the penitentiary's future. He toured the facility and told reporters he was eager to start work. As Carter announced his plans for the administration, he included many of the recommendations of the investigative committees. He told reporters from the *Jefferson City News-Tribune* that "one of our top-priority assignments should be a continuation and intensification of the in-service training for pris-on personnel." He also planned to update the classification system so that Missouri could provide more individualized treatment for inmates, which would include medical and psychiatric care as well as educational and vocational opportunities. Of course, Carter also recognized the necessity of repairing the riot damage. The legislature obliged him in this goal with $1.5 million in appropriations to sup-port the repairs.

Unfortunately, not all the committees' recommendations were heeded. Specifically, the highway patrol continued to play a role in the administration of Missouri's correctional system. When War-den Ralph Edison stepped down in 1956, Carter appointed another former highway patrolman, Elbert V. Nash, to take Edison's place. Surprisingly, Carter made this choice even though two professional prison administrators from out of state also applied and qualified for the job.

Warden Nash might have been overly optimistic about the con-ditions he would face. He told reporters from the *Jefferson City Post-Tribune* he felt "a deep seated interest in penology and social work." Additionally, Nash did not believe his background with the highway patrol would be a problem. Nash said the criticism of the patrol's influence in the state correctional system was "somewhat unwarranted."

Under Carter and Nash, some limited improvements were made. Probably the most far-reaching decision the legislature approved during this time period was the decision to begin building new cor-rectional institutions. Although more space and more modern facili-ties were desperately needed, in some ways this reform helped make conditions at the penitentiary more difficult as inmates who were less violent and more willing to cooperate in education and treat-ment programs were placed in other facilities.

This change began with the Moberly Medium Security Prison. The legislature appropriated funds for a medium security institution to help relieve overcrowding at the prison in the late 1950s. On January 17, 1963, the new prison was dedicated and began operating. Only the very best prisoners were sent to Moberly. There they participated in many educational and recreational programs. They also had substantial freedoms—they lived in dormitory-style housing and had their own keys to their rooms. While the nature of the inmates at Moberly, combined with the programs provided, created a recipe for success, the "hard core" criminals remained in the penitentiary.

Some politicians criticized the Department of Corrections for this arrangement. They believed Moberly was nothing but a showplace to please the public and argued that the penitentiary should be abandoned because it was too costly to operate and caused too much suffering to the inmates. They supported their arguments with horror stories of violence and escapes. These critics believed that the new prisons detracted public attention from the conditions at the main penitentiary.

And the conditions continued to be difficult. Violent episodes plagued the penitentiary throughout the summer of 1964. In June of that year, the administration attempted to integrate the cellblocks by moving nine black prisoners from the crumbling A Hall into cellblocks occupied exclusively by whites. One warm night, however, a dozen men with pillowcases over their heads attacked a group of black inmates as they returned to their new cells. The attackers carried improvised knives and slashed viciously at their victims, killing one.

More violence followed in August. The press blamed Director Carter and the tensions caused him to clash repeatedly with Warden Nash. Things got worse as the governor's race heated up that fall. Warren Hearnes promised during his campaign that he would reform the state's correctional system. When Hearnes was elected, Director Carter resigned, agreeing to stay only as long as it took Hearnes to find a replacement.

As the holidays approached in 1964, pressures on the administrators of the penitentiary mounted. State Representative J. J. Rabbitt, chairman of the legislative committee on correctional facilities, released a report in December, the result of another eighteen-month investigation. It demonstrated that many of the problems that had led to the riot had not been remedied. Buildings still were not receiving regular maintenance and the officers were ill-equipped to deal with the number of prisoners. The report indicated there had been over 200 acts of violence during the period of study.

When he released the report, Representative Rabbitt also suggested that Warden Nash be replaced. He told the *Jefferson City News-Tribune* that he believed Nash's replacement should be "an individual with modern correctional training." Although Nash put on a brave face for the newspapers, calling Rabbitt's suggestions "characteristic of a politician who has lost an election," he was overwhelmed by the problems facing the penitentiary.

On December 19, Warden Nash and his wife attended the employee Christmas party, and everyone thought he acted like his usual self. But as they returned home, Nash confided to his wife that "he had caused too many people too much trouble." That night he shot himself.

Colonel Carter took over the warden's position until a replacement could be found. He assured the governor that everything was under control. But the problems that had caused the 1954 riot still had not been effectively dealt with. Carter's handle on the situation continued to slip. In January 1965, Governor Hearnes took office. The budget he proposed to the legislature that spring contained a pay increase for the penitentiary guards. To further follow up on his campaign promises, Hearnes began another nationwide search for a well-trained professional to take over as director of the Department of Corrections.

This time, the politicians heeded the riot commission reports. The man they eventually hired, Fred T. Wilkinson, had spent his entire career in corrections. In the federal penitentiary system, he had held various posts, beginning as a guard and eventually becoming a warden, first of the Atlanta Penitentiary and then of Alcatraz.

Wilkinson believed in the new trends in correctional thinking. He thought that prison sentences should be short and that prisoners should receive incentives for good behavior such as offers of reductions in the time they had to serve. That is, he believed that probation and parole played a vital part in the correctional system.

Wilkinson took office on April 1, 1965, and under the influence of his theories, the penitentiary saw major improvements. Formal

Above left, "Friendly Fred" Wilkinson. After decades of violence, Time Magazine credited Fred Wilkinson with bringing the Missouri State Penitentiary "out of purgatory." In dealing with the penitentiary's problems, Wilkinson brought experience gained at Alcatraz and other federal prisons. Courtesy of Missouri State Archives.

recreation programs were offered for the first time. Baseball and softball fields were built, and an eighteen-hole mini golf course was installed. The prisoners were allowed to wear Bermuda shorts on the golf course, and *Time* magazine carried a picture of the spectacle of prisoners lining up their putts. The accompanying article lauded the recent improvements. Some prisoners appreciated the changes so much that when they earned the right to transfer to Moberly they quickly asked to be transferred back to the penitentiary because of the better opportunities for recreation.

Wilkinson had faith in the idea that proper education and treatment could save at least some criminals from themselves. This optimism fueled his leadership style. "I like to stop and chat with the inmates when they are at ease," he said in his book *The Realities of Crime and Punishment: A Prison Administrator's Testament.* This practice led many of the inmates to call him Friendly Fred.

Under Wilkinson, the Missouri Department of Corrections began to make real progress toward becoming a modern correctional system with the penitentiary as its flagship institution. This resulted in

An inmate poses next to the handball courts that were part of Wilkinson's plan to revitalize the penitentiary. Wilkinson believed in "recreation therapy." That is, he believed that sports and other recreational activities "might well be of help in diverting prison inmates from their troubles and grudges against the world." Courtesy of Missouri State Archives.

better treatment for the inmates and reduced rates of men returning to crime once they were released. But the penitentiary remained a violent place, housing the "worst of the worst" because of the increased use of alternate programs. The result was that the final decades of the penitentiary's existence demonstrated a combination of progressive improvements and surprising violence.

Inmates pause to pose for a photograph during a game of miniature golf. The addition of the miniature golf course was part of the reforms instigated by Fred Wilkinson. Courtesy of Missouri State Archives.

James Earl Ray

It's disappointing being caught.... I'd rather be ... *out there*. But it's not the end of the world. There's tomorrow. —James Earl Ray, quoted in Hampton Sides, *Hellhound on His Trail*

James Earl Ray was another infamous Missouri State Penitentiary inmate who is more famous for what he did after he left the penitentiary than for what he did while he was an inmate. Ray's ingenious escape from the Missouri State Penitentiary put him on the scene when Martin Luther King Jr. was killed. Even today, debate still rages about whether Ray was the actual killer or just a cog in a huge conspiracy. But no debate rages about how he escaped from the Missouri State Penitentiary.

James Earl Ray was born on March 10, 1928, to a poverty-stricken family in Illinois. When he was two years old, the family sought a better life in Missouri, but it was not to be. Even after purchasing a farm in 1935, crime and alcohol continued to play a major role in the family's affairs. Ray was running errands for a local brothel by the time he was fourteen years old.

Ray spent a brief period in the army but was discharged in 1948 for drunkenness and general ineptitude. He tried several jobs but was unable to make a living, and by 1960 he had accumulated a string of convictions. That year, he participated in an armed robbery in St. Louis. His conviction for that crime earned him a twenty-year sentence in the Missouri State Penitentiary.

According to historian Hampton Sides, who wrote *Hellhound on His Trail* describing the manhunt for Ray, lack of diligence was not the reason Ray had been unable to hold a steady job. In his book, Sides explains that in the penitentiary, Ray focused obsessively on escape. During Ray's tenure at the penitentiary, he made at least two escape attempts. First, he tried to climb over the wall with a homemade ladder. In another attempt, he was spotted on the roof of a building.

Inmate photograph of James Earl Ray from his time at the Missouri State Penitentiary. Courtesy of Missouri State Archives.

In his cell, Ray could often be found doing push-ups and other exercises to keep up his strength for his escape attempts. When he wasn't trying to escape, he behaved and tried to make himself as inconspicuous as possible. One prison administrator recalled, "He was just a *nothing* here."

In early 1967, his preparations took a drastic turn. He checked out travel books about Mexico and experimented with walnut dye to make his skin look darker. Ray also took up a strange new form of exercise: "He would curl himself in a tiny ball and hold the position for hours, straining to crunch his body into the tightest possible space."

On April 22, 1967, Ray went down to the prison bakery at about eight in the morning carrying what looked like a small bag of toiletries. The bag actually contained twenty candy bars and a transistor radio. Ray went to the locker room where he had hidden a set of clothes that could pass for civilian wear. He slipped on the white shirt and black pants. Then he put his prison uniform back on over the disguise so he could remain inconspicuous during the last few steps of his escape. Once he was ready, Ray went down to the loading dock and climbed into one of the large metal boxes that were used to deliver bread from the bakery at the penitentiary to other institutions in the Department of Corrections. Ray smashed down the first layer of bread and climbed in. On top of him, someone placed a false bottom before filling the rest of the space with bread.

The bread box was then loaded onto a freight truck. Before the truck could leave the premises, it had to be inspected for possible stowaways. But the guard never thought to look beyond the first layer of bread. Once Ray was sure the truck was beyond the walls of the penitentiary, he climbed out and removed his prison clothes. When the truck slowed to make a turn, he jumped out and was gone.

Ray listened to his radio as he marched west and ate his candy bars. There was no media frenzy, and the penitentiary offered only a $50 reward for his capture. After a few days, Ray began to breathe easier. He next turned up in Los Angeles where he took a bartending course under the name of Eric Galt. In March the next year, he disappeared again. His next appearance would be in Atlanta, the hometown of Martin Luther King Jr.

In Atlanta, Ray devoured newspaper articles about the famous civil rights leader. He spent hours driving around to learn the streets of Atlanta and King's routines. During this time, Ray kept a map on which he had circled the locations of his rooming house, King's residence, and King's church.

Then, in March, a new development changed Ray's plans. King publicly announced that he would lead a demonstration in support of striking garbage workers in Memphis, Tennessee. The strike had already caught national media attention, so King's announcement quickly made the news. By following newspaper and radio accounts about the plans for the demonstration, Ray learned exactly where King would be.

On April 3, 1968, both men headed to Memphis. Ray rented a room in a cheap motel called the New Rebel. King stayed in his favorite Memphis motel, the Lorraine. The next morning, Ray headed over to the Lorraine, scouting the nearby territory for a suitable hiding place. When he found the 422½ Main Street Rooming House, he knew he had found his spot. The place was a dive—rooms rented for $8 a week and one tenant later called it "a half-step up from homelessness." But to Ray it was perfect. The rooming house was just a block from King's motel, and the communal bathroom at the end of the hall provided a direct line of sight to the balcony in front of King's hotel room.

Ray paid the manager $8 and set up surveillance from his room, peering out the window with a pair of binoculars and listening to news reports on the radio he had carried with him as he escaped from the penitentiary. A few minutes before 6:00 p.m., King came out of his room at the Lorraine and stood on the balcony, waiting for his companions to gather to go to dinner. Knowing he might only have minutes, Ray rushed to the bathroom, stuck the nose of his rifle out the window, and pulled the trigger. Then he wrapped the gun and his radio in a green blanket and dashed out of the rooming house.

At the Lorraine, pandemonium ensued. Police were already on the street as Ray made his way to the white Ford Mustang he had parked nearby. Knowing the police would be suspicious of the long thin bundle he carried, Ray ditched it near a local shop. He was able to make it to his car, but the shopkeeper alerted authorities to the package.

The gun was rushed to FBI headquarters in Washington, D.C., and six quality fingerprints were recovered. FBI agents began the painstaking job of comparing the fingerprints from the gun to those of known criminals. They also began to puzzle over a number that had been partially removed from the casing of the radio.

Meanwhile, Ray made his way to Canada. In Canada, he was able to obtain a false passport. He then traveled to Europe, hoping to get connected with groups recruiting mercenaries to fight in support of apartheid in Rhodesia.

Back in Washington, the FBI had set up a situation room; agents had their meals brought in and slept on cots in the corners. The dedication paid off when they matched the fingerprints from the gun to the fingerprints on file from Ray's time at the Missouri State Penitentiary. This clue also helped them realize the importance of the numbers on the radio they had found among Ray's belongings—it had been Ray's inmate number when he was incarcerated at the Missouri State Penitentiary.

In London, Ray learned from a reporter that the best place to get information about joining Rhodesian mercenary forces was Brussels. He made plans to go there. As he left London, an immigration official noticed that Ray carried a second passport. His questions ultimately led to Ray's apprehension.

Initially, Ray thought he would have no trouble mounting a defense. Several anti–civil rights organizations, such as the Klu Klux Klan, raised money to hire top-flight lawyers for him. But in the end, the trail of evidence, including the fingerprints on the gun and the radio marked with Ray's Missouri State Penitentiary inmate number, proved more than any lawyer could beat. On March 10, 1969, Ray pleaded guilty to murder, and the judge sentenced him to serve ninety-nine years in the Tennessee Department of Corrections.

Although the crime had officially been solved, the mystery surrounding the murder of Martin Luther King Jr. remained. Ray soon claimed that his guilty plea had been false—a mysterious man named Raul had actually pulled the trigger, Ray reported—and he began working to get a new trial. He even convinced the King family that he was not the guilty party. In his spare time, he practiced his escape techniques, giving Tennessee officials a scare in 1977 and again in 1979 by escaping from the maximum security prison in which he was held. Each time he was recaptured.

In 1991, Ray published a book, *Who Killed Martin Luther King? The True Story of a Convicted Assassin*, but still the courts found there was no reason to grant a new trial. Ray's court cases and the decision of the King family to support his efforts for a new trial kept his case in the spotlight, but in the end it did not help Ray. He died in prison on April 23, 1998.

But the controversy surrounding the assassination of Martin Luther King Jr. did not die with Ray. In 2000, the U.S. Attorney General conducted another inquiry. Although the inquiry concluded that there was insufficient evidence to reopen the case, conspiracy theorists and historians alike continue to publish books and articles. Most of the investigators and attorneys involved in the case believe the evidence, including the discovery of Ray's prison radio in the same bundle as the murder weapon, is overwhelming. Thus, in a small way, Ray's time at the penitentiary helped assure that he did not get away with his horrendous crime.

The Jailhouse Lawyer

> One of the influences most disruptive of discipline and demoralizing to administration stemmed from . . . the Johnson v. Avery case . . . raised by a prisoner named Johnson who claimed that his rights were being violated because he was not permitted to act as a "jailhouse lawyer" to represent other inmates in a penitentiary. —Fred T. Wilkinson, *The Realities of Crime and Punishment*

During the last decades of the twentieth century, the story told by prison authorities seemed to indicate that things were looking up for the Missouri State Penitentiary. New opportunities for education and recreation had been added, guards and other officials received professional training, and the entire prison experience was geared toward rehabilitation. Not surprisingly, the inmates still felt they had plenty to complain about. And as the turn of the century approached, inmates found a new listener for their complaints: the courts.

It almost goes without saying that when people enter prison, they give up a number of rights. For most of this country's history, the courts accepted that truism entirely, and left prison management to the discretion of prison administrators. A series of U.S. Supreme Court decisions in the early 1970s, however, changed that view dramatically.

Drawing inspiration from the Civil Rights movement in the 1960s, inmates began filing lawsuits under a statute known as Section 1983. Section 1983 is the statutory designation in the U.S. Code for the part of the Civil Rights Act that allows a person to file a suit against the government if that person's constitutional rights have been violated. If the person wins, he or she is entitled to a monetary award to be determined by the court. During the early 1960s, prisoners started filing cases under Section 1983 in the federal courts, and the lawsuits quickly got out of hand. In 1968, the Supreme Court upheld a court of appeals opinion finding that racial segregation in prisons was unconstitutional. Later, the high court relied on that decision to determine that prisoners had a right to bring lawsuits under Section 1983 challenging other restrictions imposed by prison administrators.

This change in the law brought many challenges for administrators at the Missouri State Penitentiary. In the 1960s, inmates started using lawsuits to try to affect administrators' decisions. One inmate broke his leg during his escape out an upper-story window. While on the run, he was unable to get his leg treated. He eventually turned himself in to get treatment, but then filed a malpractice suit against the prison doctors. In 1969, seventeen Black Muslims mutinied at the penitentiary. After the mutiny was suppressed, the mutineers filed numerous court cases claiming that the punishment they received for their actions during the mutiny violated their constitutional rights.

The preparation of legal papers became a discipline problem. In his book *The Realities of Crime and Punishment: A Prison Administrator's Testament*, Fred Wilkinson reported that after the decision in *Johnson v. Avery*, a Supreme Court case stating that prisons could not prevent inmates from helping other inmates draft legal papers, the penitentiary law library became a dangerous place. "Gangs of inmates and their muscle men single out weaker prisoners and tell them they have just been assigned a jailhouse lawyer," he wrote. "For this non-service the victims are forced to pay heavily in canteen items, particularly cigarettes, and in many instances to obtain money from their mothers or other relatives to be forwarded to outside relatives of the extortionists." The rule also allowed prisoners who otherwise should have been separated to meet for such activities as planning escapes.

Of course, not all the claims were frivolous. In 1978, penitentiary inmates filed a class action suit alleging that the overcrowded and unsanitary conditions in the prison violated the constitutional protection against cruel and unusual punishment. After hearing testimony, a federal judge ruled that the overall conditions in the penitentiary were favorable. A reporter from the *Jefferson City News Tribune* summarized the judge's ruling, stating "that the stories of mice droppings, mold and roaches in the food, area, 'while occasionally true and while unappetizing, do not fairly reflect the general conditions which exist in those areas.'" The judge did find, however, that over a thousand of the prison's inmates were housed in severely overcrowded conditions. These inmates were living two to a cell in cells that had only 47 square feet of floor space. The judge ordered prison administrators to make a plan for improvement.

Penitentiary officials were generally satisfied with the judge's ruling. They believed that another round of prison building that the legislature had authorized the year before would allow them to formulate a plan that the judge would find acceptable. A week after

Two views of a cell in A-Hall. Prior to a federal court order requiring penitentiary staff to reduce overcrowding, an average of six inmates lived in each cell
this size. Later, A-Hall became an honor dorm, where inmates, now living only
one to a cell, were permitted more freedom than anywhere else. One inmate
who lived in A-Hall was permitted to keep a forty-gallon fish tank filled with
tropical fish while others decorated their walls with murals.
Photographs by the author.

the judge's initial ruling, the officials submitted their plan, and on November 21, the judge approved it. Under the plan, the penitentiary had until December 31, 1980, to eliminate the overcrowded conditions.

Throughout the 1980s, the administrators of Missouri's Department of Corrections would continue to struggle with the issue of overcrowding. Prisoners were shifted to new facilities, but changes in the criminal code including stiffer penalties for many crimes resulted in a continuing flow of new inmates. Even as the number of prisons in Missouri skyrocketed, with more inmates came increased crowding and more lawsuits.

Administrators fought back, because, as one administrator wrote, many of the lawsuits "were blatantly frivolous." Several administrative tactics were employed to help limit the disruptive nature of inmate litigation while at the same time identifying and correcting conditions that caused valid complaints.

The first major change came in how inmates at the Missouri State Penitentiary were allowed to present their complaints to the court. Some administrators believed that inmates filed lawsuits simply to get some time outside the walls to make their court appearances. Administrators were concerned about this because transportation of prisoners to court caused security risks. In the spring of 1988, the Missouri legislature passed a bill that would allow inmates to make their court appearances via closed circuit television. This allowed easier processing of inmate lawsuits where it applied, but it did not decrease the tide of claims.

That same year, the Missouri State Penitentiary began to implement a grievance procedure with the goal of helping to reduce the number of lawsuits filed. Under the grievance procedure, inmates were encouraged to report problems and get them solved informally. Initially, the complaint was subjected to a three-step review. Later, the procedure was modified to contain four steps. First, the complaint was reviewed at the prison, then it was passed to the division and finally to the director of the Department of Corrections. If none of these entities provided a satisfactory response, the inmate could then present his complaint to the Citizens Advisory Committee, which provided independent review. If the problem had not been resolved by the end of this process, the case could proceed to court.

The procedure aided prison officials in several ways. First, it allowed many complaints to be solved quickly without resorting to costly litigation. Second, if litigation was necessary, the grievance procedure aided administrators in collecting the documents and other evidence that would be needed in court. Finally, there was the potential that the program would provide another weapon in court. Federal law provided that if the procedure were certified by the federal government, any inmate who sued the prison before completing the procedure would have his lawsuit dismissed automatically. The U.S. Department of Justice certified the penitentiary's grievance procedure in 1990. The complaint procedure was later expanded to all the prisons in Missouri. By September 1991, the grievance procedure had dramatically reduced the number of inmate lawsuits.

Another improvement that helped decrease the number of lawsuits was the establishment of the Constituent Services Office. The Constituent Services Office, established in January 1994, responded to questions raised about the conditions of confinement. The office was soon responding to questions from inmates and their families as well as legislators and other government agencies. According to the *Horizon*, the Department of Corrections employee newsletter, the Constituent Services Office was a key component in reducing inmate litigation because many lawsuits had arisen out of what began as a misunderstanding of prison policy.

Of course, all these changes did not end inmates' complaints. In fact, at least one prisoner thought it made the problems worse. He said that instead of the Missouri Department of Corrections, the agency should be called the Missouri Department of Politics. Still, court orders regarding overcrowding and other prison conditions had helped improve life for prisoners at the penitentiary.

Another aspect of prison life that improved during this period was access to education. Although it took many years, administrators eventually replaced inmate tutors with certified teachers. In 1961, the school program in the penitentiary was accredited by the state Board of Education. In the report made that year, the prison administrators reported, "More men are taking advantage of the education facilities as each month passes." In the 1970s, the prison began to partner with local universities and community colleges to offer college-level classes to inmates.

The importance of education and preparation for outside life played an ever larger role in prison life during the 1980s and 1990s. Postsecondary programs expanded, and in 1995, Governor Mel Carnahan signed a law requiring that inmates obtain their GED before becoming eligible for parole.

In the late 1990s, these programs were combined with a new penological theory, which administrators called the "Parallel Universe." Recognizing that all but a very few prisoners would eventually return to society, they began to shift their focus from controlling prisoners while they were confined to preparing prisoners for release. In theory, the systems developed in the Parallel Universe transferred more control and decision-making authority to the inmates. As officials explained in *Time for Change*, the 1999 to 2000 annual report of the Department of Corrections, the Parallel Universe sought "compliance through strategies focused internally, not externally imposed." In the penitentiary, as well as the other institutions, inmates could participate in drug and alcohol abuse treatment programs, vocational training, counseling, and other activities designed to help them learn the skills necessary to participate as productive members of society.

With these advances, however, the inadequacies of the penitentiary facility itself became apparent. The old cellblocks did not provide a secure way to monitor inmates as they moved from school to work to recreation. Larger numbers of guards were needed to provide security at the penitentiary than at other institutions, with correspondingly less money available for the new programs. Additionally, moving the more tractable offenders into minimum and medium security facilities meant that the more violent ones remained in the penitentiary. This made the penitentiary itself a more violent place. Thus, ironically, improvements in the treatment of offenders began to motivate officials to begin to seriously contemplate decommissioning the oldest prison west of the Mississippi.

This is a typical classroom in the penitentiary school in the 1940s. At that time, classes were taught by inmate volunteers using donated books and materials. Courtesy of Missouri State Archives.

The End of an Era

KAI250 standing down. 168 years of tradition has ended—a new tradition begins. —Captain John Motel, quoted by Mark Schreiber, interview by author

As far back as the 1954 riot, officials knew that the old prison needed to be replaced, but problems of funding and increasing offender populations caused officials to focus on creating more prisons rather than replacing the existing penitentiary facility. It was not until 1998 that Missouri officials began to plan the closing of the Missouri State Penitentiary.

In the 1980s and 1990s, the number of prisons in Missouri exploded. By this time, officials had strict guidelines for how many prisoners could be kept in each facility. When that was combined with the rising number of offenders, the result was an almost constant stream of groundbreakings. In the late 1990s, more than one new prison opened in Missouri every year.

Still, the Department of Corrections had difficulty finding places for all the prisoners. Prisoners were kept in tents at some facilities; some prisoners were sent to other states. At least one inmate at the penitentiary thought these attempts were misguided. As with most inmates, freedom was foremost on his mind, and he wrote to the Department of Corrections newsletter *Horizon*, suggesting that prisoners be released rather than kept in tents.

Not surprisingly, officials did not embrace his suggestion. In September 2001, the Department of Corrections broke ground on the new Jefferson City Correctional Center. The facility was state of the art. The physical design of the cellblocks improved visibility so that fewer correctional officers could supervise more inmates. It was estimated that the facility would require sixty fewer employees than the penitentiary, saving Missouri taxpayers $1.5 million a year.

The decision was a tough one. Many felt the historic importance of the old facility justified the cost. But subsequent events proved that the time had come to abandon the use of the penitentiary.

At the turn of the twenty-first century, a reporter from the *Jefferson City News Tribune* described the penitentiary as "a city within a city." Seventy officers were on duty during every shift to supervise more than 1,900 of Missouri's most dangerous offenders. The walls of cells were covered with almost 200 years' worth of graffiti; the artwork of men longing for freedom contained portraits, cars, names, and even calendars. The prison yard was surrounded by twenty-five buildings that had been continually modified over the course of the prison's history. Underneath the prison, there was "a maze of electrical, plumbing and ventilation systems." This design—or lack thereof —left numerous nooks and crannies where inmates could hide and plan nefarious activities ranging from murder to escape.

Continuous maintenance was required to keep the prison operating, and by 2002, even that was not enough. On May 19, 2002, a portion of the wall collapsed. Two fences equipped with razor wire and motion detectors were quickly built to bridge the gap, and officials obtained a replacement guard tower from another Missouri correctional center. The cause of the collapse was determined to be age. Although no one was injured and no one escaped, the wall collapse helped solidify commitment to the building of a new prison.

Another problem with the old facility was the difficulty it created for supervising inmates. Jefferson City residents learned this in a visceral way in October 2002.

This aerial view of the penitentiary was taken during the 1980s. Across the bottom of the picture is the railroad and the River. In the upper left corner the ball fields and recreation areas can be seen. The large white building in the center of the photograph is the famous A Hall. Courtesy of Missouri State Archives.

On Wednesday, October 22, 2002, Chris Sims, Shannon Phillips, and Toby Viles reported for work at the prison ice house at approximately three in the afternoon. The men, all convicted of murder, had worked peacefully together in the past and were allowed to work together unsupervised, with only periodic checks by the guards. They were scheduled to work until 9:00 p.m.

At 5:30 p.m., Sims reported for dinner as usual. Prisoners often skipped meals, so the guards were not alarmed when neither Phillips nor Viles appeared. At about 6 p.m., the guards called down to check on the inmates and spoke with Viles. Nothing more was heard from the inmates for several hours.

About a half an hour after the inmates' shift was supposed to have ended, the guard on duty called the ice house to tell the inmates to return to their cells for the night. When he received no answer, investigation resulted in the discovery of Viles' body. Viles had been killed by a blow to the head. Next to the body, Sims and Phillips had left a note threatening to kill anyone who got in their way. Officials searched all night but could find no trace of Sims or Phillips.

The next morning, officials went door-to-door in Jefferson City to search for the missing inmates. The highway patrol and the Jefferson City Police Department aided in the investigation led by the Cole County Sheriff's Department. Investigators searched the inmates' cell and called their families. The cell had been stripped of anything valuable. Sims and Phillips's inmate accounts had been emptied and the resulting cash used to buy a stockpile of nonperishable food items. The inmates' families could not provide any information about the possible whereabouts of the prisoners.

For three days, the area where Viles's body had been found was cordoned off as a crime scene. Only the investigators dealing with the homicide were allowed access. On Sunday morning, however, the crime scene was cleared, and searchers began to look through the nooks and crannies of the old ice house. One officer broke through a peg board on the wall and found a hole behind it. The hole led to a space underneath a stairwell where Sims and Phillips were hiding.

Despite their threatening note, the pair surrendered quietly. Sims and Phillips, knowing that the old prison would soon be closing, had planned to stay hidden until all the inmates and officers had been transferred to the new Jefferson City Correctional Center. Then, when the prison was empty, they would make their escape. Not knowing the exact date of the planed transfer, Sims and Phillips stockpiled food in preparation for an indefinite wait.

This incident forever quieted the opposition to closing the old prison. The security risk presented by not being able to find inmates was too great. Jefferson City residents were tense during the crisis, and when it was over everyone was glad that such a situation would be much less likely in the new correctional center.

The incident also reinforced how dangerous it would be to move over a thousand criminals to the new facility. Planning began early with a campaign of misinformation. Prison officials were vague in announcing when the transition would occur. On occasion, they even

This is Guard Tower Number 8. Guards, like the one pictured above, had to be constantly alert during their shift to catch inmates attempting to scale the walls. Courtesy of Missouri State Archives.

announced false dates. Additional lights and razor wire were added to the penitentiary perimeter. Prison officials coordinated with local law enforcement to provide extra security during the transfer.

On the appointed morning, Deputy Warden of Operations Mark Schreiber arrived at the prison at 2:20 a.m. The knowledge of what was to come gave him a lonely feeling, but a small inner voice told him he had work to do, he said in an interview. Soon the prisoners were up, packing their belongings into boxes and cleaning out their cells for the last time. A Hall was now an honor unit, and so its inhabitants were the first to move. Many A Hall inmates were emotional about leaving the place where they had lived for over twenty years. Some left notes, but no one misbehaved.

Throughout the day inmates were loaded onto busses. First, the inmates were thoroughly searched and put in shackles. When each bus was full, police patrol cars escorted it to the new prison through closed streets. Several different routes were used so that no one could learn the route and thereby cause trouble. Over 5,000 boxes were required to move all the inmates' belongings.

The transfer ended ahead of schedule in the late afternoon. After the last bus arrived at the new correctional center, the officers counted the prisoners. They wanted to make sure that everyone was accounted for before the guards at the old prison left their posts. Once they had made that determination, Captain John Motel made the final radio call: "KAI250 standing down. 168 years of tradition has ended—a new tradition begins." As he said it, his voice cracked, and many of the officers found themselves without words.

Later, as the media was allowed to tour the now-empty facility with Mark Schrieber as their guide, thunder rolled and rain poured down. The group entered A Hall in darkness, and a great gust of wind blew open the windows. Standing in the rain in the historic building, Schreiber and his guests knew they were looking at the end of an era.

Ghosts?

If any place is haunted it ought to be this place. —Mark Schreiber

Even after prisoners no longer toiled away long, lonely years behind its walls, the old penitentiary still played a vital role in the cultural life of the capital city. As soon as its closure was announced, community leaders began to think about what should be done with the land and buildings. Although it was difficult for the community to reach a consensus on the correct path to take, the penitentiary had its own life. While developers haggled, the weight of history in the old buildings drew tourists to Jefferson City.

In 2001, just a short while after the Department of Corrections had announced its decision to close the penitentiary, the legislature passed an act creating the Missouri State Penitentiary Redevelopment Commission. The act provided that the commission would consist of ten members: three to be appointed by the city council of Jefferson City, three to be appointed by the county commissioners of Cole County, three to be appointed by the Missouri legislature, and a chairman selected by the governor. The commission was also given broad powers. They could buy and sell land, enter into contracts, and hire employees, all with the goal of successfully redeveloping the penitentiary property.

The first chairman of the Penitentiary Redevelopment Commission was Bill Carr, a retired St. Louis businessman. He told a reporter from the *Jefferson City News Tribune* that he saw redevelopment as a "remarkable challenge." When he took command of the Redevelopment Commission, he focused on new infrastructure, such as streets and utilities, that would be necessary before developers could make use of the site. Everyone recognized that the 147-acre site had enormous potential. The property was located close to downtown businesses and had scenic views of the Missouri River. Its history also fascinated the public.

Like any major development project, the penitentiary redevelopment began slowly with a few government office buildings. In 2002, the Department of Natural Resources began building a new headquarters on the east side of the prison property where the women's prison had been. The state also built a new Health Lab in the same area. The other major developer was also a government entity: the federal government purchased land through the Redevelopment Commission to begin work on a new federal courthouse.

During the first decade after the prison's closure, the Redevelopment Commission faced continual problems in achieving the goals the legislature had set. The legislature failed to set aside funds for planning or marketing in 2005 and 2006. The Redevelopment Commission asked for proposals from organizations willing to host tours, but the local visitor's center worried that by conducting paid tours it might lose its tax-exempt status.

In the gap, various local public safety organizations used the antiquated buildings for training. To developers, the solid old buildings represented an obstacle that had to be torn down. To firemen and police, they represented an opportunity. "The strength of these buildings creates their own challenges and opportunities. We've used tunnels and substructures to do rescue training that you wouldn't get in buildings outside the prison. These buildings have lots of nooks and crannies you can't reproduce," the Jefferson City fire chief told reporters from the *Jefferson City News Tribune* in 2008. One time the Jefferson City Police Department even brought in school children from a local elementary to help stage a training scenario for a hostage situation.

By 2009, new leadership at the Jefferson City Convention and Visitor's Bureau had solved the tax problem. They planned to offer a few hard-hat tours to test the waters; any proceeds would be used to help maintain the prison buildings, which after five years of neglect had begun to show their age. That first year, the tours quickly sold out, and the Convention and Visitors Bureau had to make waiting lists. Eventually the bureau hired an extra staff member to handle the administration of the tours. Over 3,000 tourists walked the halls of the penitentiary in 2009, learning its history from volunteers who had actually worked in the prison. By 2010, that number had increased to 11,000.

Small budgets still presented a challenge, but the increasing tour attendance demonstrated the potential that the old prison held. In 2010, Jefferson City obtained over $2 million in grants to help research and plan for development. Also in that year, the heart of the prison, the old administration building known as Housing Unit 1, was nominated for the National Register of Historic places. When it was nominated, the federal courthouse across the street was nearing completion, and one builder noted that the two buildings "create a book-end effect reflecting the history and future of government function."

In 2011, the Convention and Visitors Bureau expanded their approach to tours of the penitentiary. The bureau realized that the tours brought thousands of people to the city each year. Many of those tourists came from across the state and across the nation, and the money they spent helped to revitalize many aspects of the Jefferson City economy. The bureau began offering specialized tours. One tour focused on photography, while another allowed visitors to stay overnight and search for ghosts.

The ghost tour was prompted by the interest of visitors. During almost every standard tour, someone would ask about unusual occurrences. And they were not disappointed in the answers they received.

During a tour in 2011, a former penitentiary employee shows visitors one of the keys used to open the doors in the penitentiary. When the prison closed in 2004, it took over 900 different keys to operate all the locks on the grounds. Photograph by the author.

When the prison still operated, some guards reported hearing footsteps after all the prisoners were in their cells. When the guard would turn to look, he would see a shadowy figure that looked like it was wrapped in a blanket to keep warm. Others said Firebug Johnson still walked the halls.

These stories helped fuel the success of the ghost tours. Videos of suspected paranormal activity at the penitentiary even appeared on YouTube. On the weekend of the penitentiary's 175th anniversary, the makers of the television show *Ghost Hunters* filmed an episode on the grounds. The ghost tours were so successful, in fact, that the visitor's bureau started an overnight tour, where for $100, the stout of heart can spend the night in the penitentiary to increase the odds that they will see a ghost.

For the less adventurous, the basic two-hour tour still provides plenty of thrills. The tour begins on Lafayette Street, just outside the entrance to the penitentiary. Visitors gather in front of the imposing stone façade of Housing Unit 1, the same façade that greeted inmates for many years. While visitors wait for the tour to begin, they have to sign a waiver in case of injury because some of the prison buildings can be dangerous. The combination of the waiver and the tall stone walls creates a sense of adventure.

Once everyone has arrived, the tour guide pulls out a ring of large brass keys and opens the gate. Inside, years of neglect have caused the paint to peel, and strips of dried paint hang down like stalactites. The thick stone walls insulate the interior space, so even on warm spring days, visitors are greeted with a chill. The outside gate clangs shut, and another opens toward the inside of the penitentiary, allowing the visitors their first view of the main yard.

The yard is much less sinister than the interior of the buildings. Open grassy spaces dotted with trees separate institutional-style buildings. Aside from the tall limestone walls visible through the gaps between the buildings and the bars on the windows, it could be the campus of a community college.

After allowing a moment to look around, the tour guides lead the visitors to the penitentiary's most famous building: A Hall. Inside, three tiers of cells look down on a central hall. The tour guides explain a bit about the history of the building, including its role in the 1945 riot. During that time, it was the cellblock for African American prisoners and as many as six men were crammed into each small cell. Despite the horrible conditions, they refused to participate in the riot.

Tourists gather for a tour sponsored by the Jefferson City Convention and Visitors Bureau. Each tour is led by a former penitentiary employee, and proceeds are used to help preserve the historic buildings. Photograph by the author.

After the history lesson, visitors can explore the building. The extremely brave can take a trip to the basement to see the isolation cells. The tour guides turn out the lights so visitors can get a feel of what it might have been like to have been confined in one of the punishment cells.

Finally, the tour guides give the visitors directions on how to get to the "death house" or execution chamber on the far east side of the area enclosed by the walls. As visitors approach the building, the tour guides explain how the death house was built using inmate labor during the 1930s. Inside, visitors must divide into small groups—the rooms of the death house are not big enough to accommodate more than a few people at a time. On the south side of the building, a short hallway leads to a cell where the condemned inmates spent their

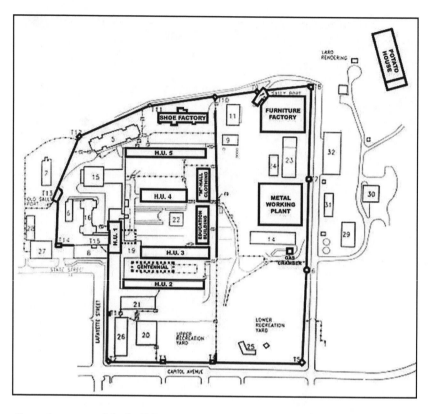

Above is a map of the buildings and walkways of the penitentiary as they currently exist. The building marked H.U. 4 in the center is the famous A-Hall. Courtesy of State of Missouri Division of Facilities Management, Design and Construction.

final hours, a control room, and the gas chamber itself. Again, brave visitors have a chance for a thrill. Anyone who dares may sit in the gas chamber and a guide will even close the door for a minute or so. On the north side of the building, there is an observation room with windows into the gas chamber. The short tour allows visitors to get a feel for the conditions prisoners faced and to learn a little about the penitentiary's long, storied history.

Much of the penitentiary's history was not pretty. Administrators constantly struggled to balance the competing demands of keeping costs down while providing to inmates legitimate opportunities for reform. This struggle meant that during its heyday, the penitentiary was populated by rough men who were forced to live in even rougher circumstances. Some, like Sonny Liston and Pretty Boy Floyd, became legends. Others were lost to the sands of time. Collectively, though, through redevelopment that respects the history of the Missouri State Penitentiary, their stories will help make improvements to the way Missouri deals with those who violate the laws. And hopefully, one day, Missouri will be able to say that any unnecessary suffering of the inmates of the Missouri State Penitentiary was not in vain.

For More Reading

American Prisons: A History of Good Intentions, by Blake McKelvey (Montclair, NJ: P. Smith, 1977), and *The Discovery of the Asylum: Social Order and Disorder in the New Republic*, by David J. Rothman (New Brunswick, NJ: Aldine Transaction, 2002), provide an excellent overview of the history of American prisons and the development of the penitentiary system.

The definitive history of the Missouri Department of Corrections is *Somewhere in Time: 170 Years of Missouri Corrections*, by Mark S. Schreiber and Laura Burkhardt Moeller (Marceline, MO: Walsworth Publishing, 2004). The Missouri State Penitentiary figures prominently in this book because it was the flagship institution for the department. The book provides a comprehensive chronicle of the department's history from the founding of the Missouri State Penitentiary until 2004.

Several informative essays about various aspects of the penitentiary appear in the two-volume work *Heartland History: Essays on the Cultural Heritage of the Central Missouri Region*, by Gary Kremer (St. Louis: Third Street Books, 2000). Kremer discusses escapes, prison labor, and the career of Sonny Liston.

The most detailed account of life in the Missouri State Penitentiary during the middle of the nineteenth century is *Prison Life and*

Reflections; Or, A Narrative of the Arrest, Trial, Conviction, Imprisonment, Treatment, Observations, Reflections and Deliverance of Work, Burr and Thompson Who Suffered an Unjust and Cruel Imprisonment in Missouri Penitentiary for Attempting to Aid Some Slaves to Liberty, by George Thompson (New York: S.W. Benedict, 1848). This book is available free from Google Books. It details how George Thompson was tried and convicted of attempting to help slaves to freedom before providing a chronicle of his years in the penitentiary.

There are numerous sources about Kate Richards O'Hare. *Rebel against Injustice: The Life of Frank P. O'Hare*, by Peter H. Buckingham (Columbia: University of Missouri Press, 1996), has an excellent description of the circumstances surrounding the speech for which Kate Richards O'Hare was prosecuted as well as a detailed account of her trial. O'Hare's own description of her experiences at the penitentiary was published in *In Prison*, by Kate Richards O'Hare (Seattle: University of Washington Press, 1976).

For more details about Bonny Heady Brown, see *Zero at the Bone: The Playboy, the Prostitute, and the Murder of Bobby Greenlease*, by John Heidenry (New York: St. Martin's Press, 2009).

For more information about the death penalty in Missouri, see *Death Sentences in Missouri, 1803–2005: A History and Comprehensive Registry of Legal Executions, Pardons, and Commutations*, by Harriet C. Frazer (Jefferson, NC: McFarland & Co., 2006), and *The Execution Protocol: Inside America's Capital Punishment Industry*, by Stephen Trombley (New York: Crown Publishers, 1992). Frazer's book has extensive coverage of the topic from the earliest European settlement of the area that would become Missouri with emphasis on the people who were executed. The book gives a detailed account of many executions. Trombley discusses the development of Missouri's execution procedures during the late 1980s and early 1990s.

A very readable biography of Charles "Pretty Boy" Floyd is *The Life and Death of Pretty Boy Floyd*, by Jeffery S. King (Kent, OH: Kent State University Press, 1998).

For more information about James Earl Ray, see *Hellhound on His Trail: The Stalking of Martin Luther King Jr. and the International Hunt for His Assassin*, by Hampton Sides (New York: Doubleday, 2010).

The Realities of Crime and Punishment: A Prison Administrator's Testament, by Fred T. Wilkinson (Springfield, MO: Mycroft Press, 1972), describes Wilkinson's theory of criminal justice and how correctional institutions should be run. As this theory was based on his years as a prison administrator, including service as the director of the Missouri Department of Corrections in the late 1960s, his description contains many vignettes about inmates from the Missouri State Penitentiary.

Index

About the Author

Jamie Pamela Rasmussen is an adjunct instructor in the Department of Criminology and Criminal Justice at Missouri State University. She lives in Springfield, Missouri.